RAFFLES

Thomas Stamford Raffles was born aboard his father's ship on its return from America during the War of Independence. At 14, Raffles became a clerk in the East India Company's headquarters in London where his industry and intelligence attracted attention, leading to his appointment as assistant to the Chief Secretary in Penang, and an increase in salary from £70 to £1,500 per annum.

Marrying a widow ten years his senior before leaving for the Far East, Raffles' personal tenderness and warmth made him a humanist in public affairs. His abilities brought him to the attention of Lord Minto, Governor General in India, who made Raffles his adviser on the invasion of Java. Raffles became the first Lieutenant-Governor and set about reforming the Dutch administration methods. Raffles was a keen historian, linguist and botanist, and on his return to England brought thousands of plants. On his first return, stopping to meet Napoleon at St Helena, Raffles was lionized by London society and knighted by the Regent.

The foundation of Singapore was an involved and by no means universally approved decision; Maurice Collis charts the political chicanery with his consummate skill in producing eminently readable prose. Raffles' retirement due to ill health and his shabby treatment by the East India Company provide a sad conclusion to his life, relieved by Raffles' continuing cultural interests and his founding of the London Zoological Gardens.

Maurice Collis was born in Ireland in 1889. He entered the Indian Civil Service and was posted to Burma, returning in 1934 to a successful literary career in England. He published thirty-five books, besides being an art critic and reviewing exhibitions. He retained a strong interest in Burma and maintained his relationship through successive prime ministers.

Jan Morris has written many celebrated books of travel and history, including the trilogy *Pax Britannica, Heaven's Command* and *Farewell the Trumpets* about the British Empire. She has long been an admirer of Maurice Collis's writing.

RAFFLES

Maurice Collis

Introduction by Jan Morris

CENTURY
LONDON MELBOURNE AUCKLAND JOHANNESBURG

First published in 1966

This edition first published in 1988 by Century,
an imprint of Century Hutchinson Ltd,
Brookmount House, 62–65 Chandos Place, London WC2N 4NW

Century Hutchinson Australia Pty Ltd,
PO Box 496, 16–22 Church Street, Hawthorn, Melbourne,
Victoria 3122, Australia

Century Hutchinson Group New Zealand Limited,
PO Box 40–086, Glenfield, Auckland 10, New Zealand

Century Hutchinson South Africa (Pty) Ltd,
PO Box 337, Bergvlei, 2012 South Africa

British Library Cataloguing in Publication Data

Collis, Maurice
  Raffles.
  I. Title
  918.1'1045   F2546

ISBN 0-7126-1927 5

Printed in Great Britain by
Richard Clay (The Chaucer Press) Ltd, Bungay, Suffolk.

Affectionately dedicated

to the

HON. JAMES AND LADY JEAN BERTIE

ACKNOWLEDGEMENTS

No one can write a book on Raffles without acknowledging a debt to C. E. Wurtzburg, whose *Raffles of the Eastern Islands* was published in 1954. His book is invaluable because it contains lavish quotations from the original authorities. Its length, however, makes it unsuitable for the general reader, as it runs to nearly 800 pages and must contain about a quarter of a million words. Nevertheless, all authors writing on Raffles subsequent to Wurtzburg are dependent on him, especially for chronology and documentation.

Mildred Archer of the India Office Library has been of great assistance to me in finding most of the illustrations here, the originals of which are in the India Office Library. I am very grateful for her kindness and industry. Clifford Musgrave was also very helpful in selecting for me from the great store of pictures, drawings and prints in the Royal Pavilion at Brighton, numbers 22 and 23.

I am also indebted to Dorothy Woodman for lending me some notes of her own concerned with Raffles's last days in London and matters subsequent to his death, all valuable details from her own researches.

CONTENTS

Contents

Contents

Contents

Contents

Contents

MAPS

INTRODUCTION

It is a pity to my mind that when Thomas Stamford Raffles, the founder of Singapore, was knighted by his friend the Prince Regent in 1817, he chose to be dubbed Sir Stamford. Tom Raffles was much more his style. He was a man of stature but not of pomp, a humanist, 'an easy man' as Lord Melbourne would have said, who lived not by the advantages of consequence, but by intellect, charm and imagination. He was, one might say, an artist in public affairs; and more particularly, he was perhaps the most fastidious and compassionate of all the remarkable men who made the British Empire, and thereby permanently altered the world.

In his time the word 'imperialist' had hardly been coined, and the Empire itself was a somewhat inchoate conception. The American colonies had been lost (Cornwallis surrendered at Yorktown in the year of Raffles' birth), and Britain was left with an indeterminate scattering of possessions across the globe — in Canada, in the West Indies, in Australia, in the West Indies, strewn among the oceans, and above all in and around the sub-continent of India.

Victorianism, soon to be born, would bring to this dominion a sense of structure and conviction. The eighteenth-century Empire had been essentially a commercial venture: the nineteenth- was to acquire altogether different ideological and even religious meanings, and was to nurture a

succession of commanding, sometimes monstrous person-
alities. There were soldiers of brutal zeal, administrators like
Old Testament patriarchs, statesmen dedicated to the
exertion of Britain's will throughout the world, and at their
head a monarch of such determined values that in later years
they would actually be named after her.

The best-known thing named after Raffles (unless you
count a character in detective fiction) was the hotel where
they invented the gin sling. He was anything but a Victorian
— was in fact quintessentially Regency Man. Born in 1781 to
modest enough origins (his father was an impecunious sea-
captain), he made his way in the world by the virtues of the
time — reason, panache, gracefulness, supplemented by a fair
share of social opportunism. He was never an Establishment
man, or a man of convention. He was as courteous and
welcoming to his servants as he was to his aristocratic patrons,
and when he married Sophia, his second wife, to live with her
happily ever after, he affectionately described her as
possessing 'neither rank, fortune nor beauty'.

For Maurice Collis, the author of this long-admired
biography, Raffles provided a perfect subject; Collis himself
was an Englishman of urbane tastes, attracted by the more
exotic kinds of elegance, sympathetic to originals and blessed
with a style which, though of a deceptive simplicity, is really
as exquisitely cast and polished as a piece of Georgian silver.

It happened that Raffles entered the public service at a
climactic moment of history. Mankind was poised, as it were,
between Ages. Britain's victories in the Napoleonic wars had
left her the dominant power of the world, and had given her
incomparable Navy mastery of all the oceans. She was
destined now to usher in the Age of Technology, and Thomas
Stamford Raffles was destined, if only posthumously, to be its
major-domo in the farthest East.

He first went out in 1805 as a lesser administrator of the East India Company, in whose service he was to remain for the rest of his working life. By then most of the world had already been touched by the dynamic expansionism of the Europeans. Only the Far East was almost entirely uncolonized and unexploited: the ancient civilizations of China and Japan remained immune to western corrosions, contemptuous of western pretensions. It was as though a line had been drawn around the southern limits of the China seas, beyond which European civilization must not advance.

Maurice Collis was not given to hyperbole, and he is not I think exaggerating when he writes that the breaching of that line created the modern world – made a putative unity of it at last, and for the first time enabled the predominant cultures of east and west to size each other up. To this epochal development Raffles made a contribution specific, absolute and irreversible.

Of course it would have happened anyway — he was only the instrument of inexorable geo-political forces — but that it happened in the way it did was due directly to his force of character. Posted to Java at a time when suzerainty over the East Indies was disputed by Britain and the Netherlands, he very soon realized that the Indonesian archipelago, and in particular the islands of the Malacca Straits, could be the key to domination of the China seas. For generations western merchants had been trading with China, but they had done so only on sufferance, kept at arm's length by the preposterously self-satisfied and xenophobic Manchus. A power base at the southern end of the Indo-Chinese land mass, Raffles perceived, would enable the British to enter those regions on their own terms, bringing with them their own benefits.

For he was far more than a mere patriotic expansionist. He believed in his country as the chief agent of human progress.

An admirer of Napoleon (though cruelly disillusioned when he met the exiled Emperor on St Helena), he thought with Beethoven that the torch of Enlightenment had passed now to Great Britain. Opening the China seas to British power would open them to trade certainly, but also to ideas, arts, sciences and the example of fair Government. Raffles knew very well that he was engaged in shifting the balance of the hemispheres. 'They say', he wrote to a friend, 'I am a Spirit that will never allow the East to be quiet': and they were right.

The morality of imperialism was seldom questioned then. Raffles never fired a shot in anger, or took part in any military campaign, but he seems to have seen nothing wrong in the forcible extension of British power over alien peoples. He regarded it as a duty, like the duty of the English landowner he eventually became, to be fulfilled in as gentlemanly a way as possible. He detested slavery — William Wilberforce was one of his closest friends — and he despised the overbearing imperial manners of Britain's rivals in the Far East, the Dutch.

But then his was an open mind, and to such a sensibility crude despotism must always be distasteful. Collis says that Raffles was never bored. He was interested in almost everything — in languages, in history, and most of all in nature. He loved animals, as he loved his children, with a passionate intensity. If his founding of the London Zoo, in later life, is not his noblest claim to fame among animal-liberationists like me, I think it safe to claim that if he were alive today he would abhor the very notion of creatures in captivity.

Raffles was a self-educated man, his schooling having ended when he was fourteen, and perhaps as a result the enthusiasm of his learning was prodigious. His *History of Java* would alone have made him famous, and his great collections of orientalia enormously increased the sum of human knowledge. His town plan for Singapore was as practical as it was shapely; his prose was, as one might expect, clear and rhythmic.

One does not, however, build an Empire by kindness, scholarship or good taste. Raffles was also an extremely bold operator, of the Nelson kind. Collis considers him constitutionally unsuited to be a subordinate. He was ready to disobey orders when necessary, he had a wonderful eye for the main chance, and his sense of history told him infallibly when a risk was worth the taking.

One grand risk in particular: acquiring the island of Singapore, more or less on his own initiative, almost by sleight of hand, was Raffles' personal imperial coup. As he foresaw it opened the eastern seas first to British power, then to the full flood of Western enterprise, and it made him unique in the history of British imperialism as the only begetter of a colony. His time in Singapore was in fact brief — he spent far longer in Penang and Java — but he is honoured still in the Lion City as no other Western imperialist is honoured in the East. Neither the discrediting of the imperial idea, nor the ignominious defeat of the British in 1941, nor the rise of Singapore as an independent city-state, have extinguished the respect, now hazing into myth, with which Raffles is recalled in the city of his creation.

Raffles was cheerful by temperament, and he had a gift for enjoyment, but all in all his life was a sad one. He lost a wife and three children in his own lifetime. His own health was fragile and he died (in 1826) when he was only forty-five. Petty and malignant enemies plagued him all his life. He was shabbily treated by his employers. A mere handful of mourners, Collis tells us, attended his funeral in Hendon parish church — the fashionable world ignored it and the vicar refused to allow a memorial plaque in the church. Far from becoming Governor-General of India, as he apparently once hoped, Raffles had ended his official career as Lieutenant-Governor of the soon-to-be-abandoned and now all-but-forgotten outpost of Bencoolen.

It is one of the achievements of this book that it projects, nevertheless, a sense of happiness. One does not often feel of a public figure that his virtue really was its own reward, but one feels it of Raffles, a truly honourable and delightful man. Collis employs hyperbole only once more in his biography, and justifiably again. Quoting the ecstatic admiration for Raffles expressed by a Malay servant, he says that nowhere in the annals of the eastern Empire can be found 'so profoundly moving a testimony as this of an Asiatic's love for an Englishman'.

I have no way of knowing if this is true, but it can certainly be said that few other figures of imperial history are remembered as vividly for the attraction of their character as for their historical achievements. Raffles once said the British Empire should aspire to write its story 'in characters of light', and Maurice Collis might well have had the phrase in mind, when he illuminated Sir Stamford's own memory in this gentle sparkling work.

Jan Morris, 1987

Chapter One

THE START OF RAFFLES'S CAREER

The birth of Raffles – The slave trade and anti-slave trade movement – Raffles's position in his period – appointed clerk in the East India House – The East India Company – Bonaparte and his eastern ambitions – Raffles educates himself – appointed assistant secretary in new Presidency of Penang – marries Olivia Fancourt

Thomas Stamford Raffles was born on 6 July 1781 on board the West Indiaman *Ann* (260 tons, 4 guns), the master of which was his father, Captain Benjamin Raffles. At the time the *Ann* was three or four days out from Jamaica on the way home to England in a convoy of some two hundred vessels. The War of American Independence was at its height, and British merchantmen had to be protected against the warships both of the revolted colonists and their allies, the French and the Dutch. That same year in October the English army surrendered at Yorktown. American independence was won. Thus the birth of Raffles, destined to open the Far East to Britain, coincided with the close of her western dominion. Moreover, the victory of the Americans in their fight for liberty was the prelude to the 1789 revolution in France, so that 1781 may be seen as the year when the modern history of Europe began, the Europe which was to pervade and transform the Far East, after Raffles had opened the door.

The presence of the *Ann* in Jamaican waters touched another matter relevant to Raffles's future. The Caribbean in 1781 was the main slave market, the centre of the British slave trade since 1713 when the British became the leading slave merchants in the world after emerging victorious from the War of the Spanish Succession. The years 1780 to 1790 were, in fact, the boom years for the slave trade. Liverpool ships made some nine hundred round trips in these ten years, carrying 3,000 slaves, who were sold for fifteen million pounds. The slaves were sometimes taken direct from Africa and sometimes via Liverpool. West Indiamen, after landing them in the Caribbean, loaded up for the return voyage with the products of the islands – rum, cotton, sugar and tobacco – making thus a double profit. Such was the lucrative trade in which Raffles's father was engaged when his son Thomas was born. The anti-slave agitation was, however, about to begin, one aspect of the humanism of the period. The young Raffles grew up under its influence. His life was to cover the most momentous years of English history. In the course of it occurred such capital events as the rise of Napoleon Bonaparte to the dictatorship of Europe, the battle of the Nile which prevented him from extending his dominion over Asia, the battle of Trafalgar which established the supremacy of the British fleet over the waters of the world, the battle of Waterloo where the French met a defeat which determined the course of European history in the nineteenth century, and his own foundation of Singapore, which set the stage for nineteenth-century Asia. As its founder Raffles stands among the great figures of the age. During his time in Asia, from 1805 until 1824, he was unquestionably the leading British intellect and personality there. Lucky in that great oppor-

tunities for distinguishing himself came his way, he was unlucky in that his achievements were not fully recognized.

Extremely little is known about what happened to him
between his birth in 1781 and when in 1795, aged fourteen,
he entered the East India House (the headquarters of the East
India Company) in Leadenhall Street, London, as a clerk.
His father, though engaged in so paying a business as the
Caribbean trade, was improvident or unfortunate, lost his
money and became heavily in debt. In 1793 the young Raffles,
aged twelve, had been sent as a boarder to a school in
Hammersmith (then a village) but presently his father found
himself unable to pay the school fees and the fourteen-year-old
boy had to leave school and take the job at East India House.

The East India Company was the most extraordinary English company that has ever existed. Founded by Elizabeth in
1599 and given the monopoly of the East-West trade, it
became by force of circumstances the paramount power in
India. It was both a company and a government and till 1784
was largely independent of the British government.

In 1784 William Pitt, the twenty-four-year-old Prime
Minister, carried his India Bill which set up in London a
Board to oversee the Company. This Board of Control, a
department of the ministry, was given the power of guiding
the Court of Directors, the governing body of the East Indian
Company, in matters of major policy. Patronage was left in
the hands of the Court, though the Governors General and
the Commanders in Chief were appointed by the Board,
after consulting the Court. The government of India became
thus a joint undertaking, though it was not until 1813 that the
sovereignty of the Crown was extended over the Company's
territories and it lost its trade monopoly.

Such was the organization in which Raffles in 1795
was enlisted through his father's inability to pay for his

education. It is interesting to note that among the clerks in the East India House was Charles Lamb, the future essayist. He was six years older than Raffles and had been in the East India House for two years, where he remained for thirty-three and wrote the whole of his *œuvre*.

The year 1795–6 was a year of fate. It saw the rise of the young Bonaparte, who was then twenty-six. Leading a revolutionary army he invaded Italy and won his first dramatic victory at the bridge of Lodi, an event which inspired later the Italian poet Carducci to the famous lines:

'Quando su'l dubbio ponte tra i folgori
passava il pallido còrso.'

The tremendous drama of the pale Corsican had started. Of his early victories in Italy he said afterwards to his entourage in St. Helena: 'From that time I saw what I might become. I already saw the world beneath me as if I were being carried through the air.'* By 1799, aged thirty, he was dictator of France under the title of First Consul; in 1804 he was crowned Emperor, and was master of Europe. His ambition was to make himself also master of Asia and turn the British out of India. At St. Helena his chief regret was that he had not pushed East after his conquest of Egypt. 'Had I taken Acre I would have gone to India. I should have assumed the turban at Aleppo and headed an army of 200,000 men. Had I done so I would still be Emperor of the East.' But the British fleet, which had defeated him at the Nile in 1798 and was to defeat him in 1805 at Trafalgar, baulked that ambition. Nevertheless, the shadow of Napoleon lay over Asia till Waterloo in 1815. The pattern of Raffles's career was determined by these world events. When he entered the East India House in 1795 they had begun to unfold themselves,

* *Napoleon, The Last Phase*, by Lord Rosebery, p. 198.

but there was not the smallest indication that he was to play a distinguished part in them. After a short period of probation he was confirmed in his appointment at a salary of £70 per annum, which I suppose had the purchasing power of £500 a year today. Two years later his father died, leaving his widow and daughters, of whom there seems to have been five, with no money. The family lived on Raffles's £70. This made him, at the age of sixteen, the main support of his mother and sisters. For ten years he shouldered this responsibility with little or no rise in salary. He became aware, as a young man of talent and character may become aware, that his abilities would enable him to rise from the position of a clerk, if he could give himself the education which a father in the ordinary way would have paid for. While he must do his routine work at the East India House in a manner to win the approval of his seniors, he would have to dedicate every moment of leisure outside the office to reading as widely as possible and to the study of a second language. With the resolution of the born scholar and of a youth deeply interested in everything that books could tell him, he used to sit up till all hours working, noting, learning, and found that he was able to grasp by his unaided efforts what boys of his age had to have drilled into them. His assiduity kept him up so late that, according to the story, his mother, pressed as she was for money, remonstrated with him over his extravagance with candles. One is reminded of the anecdotes in Chinese literature of poor students struggling to qualify for the mandarinate examinations, of Ch'e Yun, for instance, of the fourth century who, unable to afford a candle, studied the classics by the fitful gleam of fireflies.

Raffles's extraordinary industry did not pass unnoticed. Willing, energetic, sensible and far better informed than the other clerks (with the exception, perhaps, of Charles Lamb), he attracted the attention of William Ramsay, the head of the office, who made a friend of him, inviting him to his house where he met persons of social consequence, a circle where the affairs of the day, at no time more exciting than at that moment, were debated. The authorities thus had their eye on Raffles, though year after year he continued as clerk with the same salary.

In 1805, however, his chance came. He was twenty-three years of age and had been in Company employ for ten years, when the world situation obliged the Board of Control to take measures in the East to strengthen the Company's China trade route. As things stood, Calcutta merchants trading with Canton had no intermediate port where they might refit, or take refuge from French warships, for the French, having occupied Holland, had taken possession of the Dutch East Indies and so lay on the flank of the Straits of Malacca, the gateway to the China Sea. At the northern entry to the Straits the Company possessed the island of Penang, which had been ceded to it in 1786 by the Sultan of Kedah, the Malay state opposite to it on the mainland, in consideration of an annual payment of 6,000 dollars. It had also come into possession in 1795 of Malacca, which was taken from the Dutch to prevent it falling into French hands. Malacca was better situated than Penang, being some hundreds of miles further into the Straits, and was a fortress with a long history from Portuguese times. But as the Company apprehended that at the close of the wars in Europe Malacca might very well have to be returned to Holland in any general settlement in Europe, it was planned to concentrate on Penang, make it, like Calcutta, Madras and Bombay, subordinate to the Governor-General in India, and fortify it. Hitherto it had not been fortified. When Arthur Wellesley, the future Duke of Wellington, inspected it in 1796, he reported that 'one hostile frigate could insult it'.

Raffles Goes to Penang

Accordingly in 1805 the Board of Control, in consultation with the Court of Directors, made Penang a Presidency. The Honourable Philip Dundas was appointed governor and was provided with a small Council. Secretaries to the Council had to be found and it was at this point that Raffles had his stroke of luck. He was chosen from among the clerks in the East India House as the most suitable man for the post of assistant to the Chief Secretary. This meant a jump in salary from some £70 per annum to £1,500. The appointment also opened for him wide opportunities (wider than he could have imagined at the time) and a life more exciting for a young man of 24 than a clerkship in Leadenhall Street.

At this time, a Mrs Olivia Fancourt called at East India House to apply for a pension, on being advised that she was entitled to one as the widow of Surgeon J. C. Fancourt, a member of the Madras establishment who had died in 1800. She was granted a donation of twenty-five guineas and a daily allowance of one shilling and threepence. Raffles became acquainted with her on this occasion. She was thirty-four, ten years older than he, a dark, striking-looking woman, intelligent and lively. Raffles took to her at once and, as his new appointment enabled him to marry, proposed and was accepted. The marriage took place in March 1805, a month before he left with her for Penang on the same ship as Dundas and the rest of the staff of the new Presidency.

Chapter Two

THE FIRST DAYS AT PENANG

Raffles and Olivia, their characters – Description of Penang – State of Oriental studies – Raffles shows himself to be very able secretary – is promoted – Meeting with John Leyden

Raffles was by nature tender, a trait which was to make him in his public capacity a humanist and in private life a great family man. He was devoted to his mother and sisters, one of whom he took with him to Penang; he provided for his mother and the other sisters before leaving. His devotion to Olivia was steady and deep. That she was ten years his senior, though a cause of remark at the time, was not unsuitable, for he was more grown-up at twenty-four than are most young men of that age, though the period was noted for precocious genius, Pitt, Bonaparte, Shelley, Keats, for instance. With ten years' experience of the East India Company's affairs, well read and by now with a fluent knowledge of French (for among his many gifts was that of languages), he was as educated as if he had taken a university degree. Olivia was better suited to him than a girl of twenty would have been. It came to be believed that between the death of her late husband, Surgeon Fancourt, in May 1800 and her marriage to Raffles in March 1805, she had been the inamorata of Thomas Moore, the poet, who addressed to her 'many of his amatory elegies' as Lord Minto put it in a letter to his wife dated May 1811. This is possible, as Thomas Moore was twenty-six in 1805, two years older than Raffles. Whatever may be the truth of this romantic tradition, it is certain that Olivia was a clever and fascinating woman. For the next ten years she was to make Raffles very happy, and her early death in Java in 1814 was a great grief to him.

During the voyage out to Penang, which took from April to September 1805, Raffles learnt Malay, the Oriental language it would be most useful for him to know, and which nobody else on the staff of the new Presidency knew or had any intention of learning. (Raffles was always ahead of his contemporaries.)

Penang at this time was known in England as Prince of Wales Island, in compliment to George III's son, not yet Regent, as his father was still sane, a popular prince nicknamed the First Gentleman of Europe, because of his looks, his clothes and his manners. The island was separated from the Malayan mainland by a strait of from one to three miles in breadth; had a range of mountains from north to south, the peaks up to 2,000 feet; was covered with splendid huge trees and had entrancing views. The temperature, much less than Calcutta's, was pleasant, but the place was not as healthy as it looked, at least for Europeans, who at that date had small knowledge of or remedy for tropical diseases. Its length was fifteen and breadth ten miles and it was largely uninhabited outside the one town, called George Town, which lay on a point of land jutting into the strait, there hardly more than a mile wide. For a Calcutta European it was the back of beyond with few of the amusements available in the other Presidency towns. The native inhabitants amounted to thirty thousand, two-thirds of them Chinese settlers, the rest Malaya, with labourers from South India, for the Malays had the sort of objection to labour which people have whose wants are simple and whose fertile lands amply supply them with food. There was one road, some ten miles long, used for drives in the cool of the evening and smooth enough for 'buggies or little phaetons', as Lord Minto later wrote, drawn by ponies from Sumatra 'the smallest fairy-like horses you ever saw'. The European inhabitants numbered just over a hundred. At that date no games like tennis or golf or polo existed to pass the time after office. Besides the evening drives on the bit of road, there were dinner parties, dances, amateur theatricals and amateur concerts. In short, it was a very dull place, made duller for a person with Raffles's intellectual interests by the indifference of the European community in general to the panorama of Oriental life. Eastern thought, history, religion, art, languages, botany, zoology, indeed everything pertaining to Asia except trade, did not interest them.

In spite of the English having been in the East for two hundred years, and before them the Portuguese for a hundred years, in spite of the voyages of the great adventurers, the exploits of the Dutch among the East Indian islands, the exploration of the South Seas by such seamen as Cook, and such embassies to the Court of China as Lord Macartney's in 1793, western information about the eastern half of the world was elementary. Burma, though adjacent to India, was hardly known except for the visit of Major Symes of His Majesty's 76 Regiment as envoy in search of trade concessions. He had published in 1800 an account of his experiences. John Crawfurd had not yet been to Siam; hardly anything was known of the Sultanates of Malaya, those exotic little courts beyond the mangrove swamps of the river mouths. The Dutch, though they claimed to have occupied Sumatra, Java and the Moluccas, knew so little of the hinterland that they had not

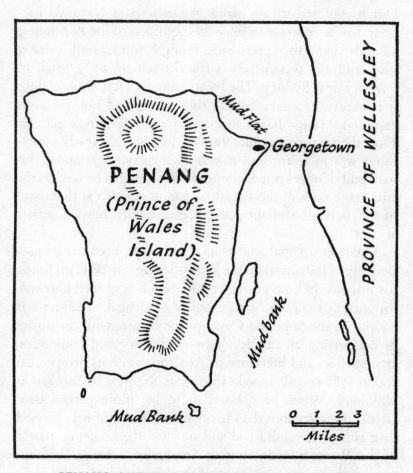

PENANG AND THE PROVINCE OF WELLESLEY
(MALAYAN MAINLAND)

discovered the greatest artistic monument of the Javanese past, the stupa of Borobudur. No Europeans, except the few Dutch confined to the island of Deshima in Nagasaki harbour, had been to Japan since the expulsion of the Portuguese a hundred and fifty years back. Hong Kong was still a desert isle; Australia was merely a convict settlement, a patch of territory near Sydney. The local bushmen were shot at sight It is hardly necessary to add that Africa had not yet been explored. Mungo Park's journey up the Niger took place in 1806, the year after Raffles's arrival in Penang. Nearly everything was to learn; and it was to the investigation of this vast field of new knowledge, and how it might be used to the advantage both of the British and (a novel idea at that date) of the native inhabitants, that Raffles applied himself almost at once.

A start in oriental studies had, of course, been made, particularly in India, and on the linguistic side. Sir William Jones, for instance (whose portrait by Reynolds is so well known), founded in 1784 the Asiatic Society of Bengal, when he was a judge in the Supreme Court of Judicature, with the object of conducting an inquiry 'into the history and antiquities, arts, sciences and literature of Asia' (to quote its prospectus) and in 1787 revealed the key position occupied by Sanskrit in philology. When he declared it to be 'more perfect than Greek, more copious than Latin and more exquisitely refined than either', he astonished and shocked the academic world of the West. In 1785 another Orientalist, Charles Wilkins, published the first translation of the Bhagavad-gita, the Song Celestial, the Sanskrit classic where the metaphysic of Hinduism has matchless expression. In 1801 this same Wilkins, after being invalided home, was put in charge of the East India Company's library in East India House, Leadenhall Street. As Raffles was with him in the same building for four years, it may safely be assumed that they met and that Raffles was stimulated and encouraged by this pioneer orientalist of fifty-two.

On arrival at Penang, however, Raffles's first duty was to justify his appointment as assistant secretary by applying himself to current business. Everything else would have to be done after dark or in the early morning, though, as he had faith in his star, and was very ambitious, he guessed it would not be unpaid overtime in the long run. Such studious habits entailed a neglect of the social round. He could not be in and out of people's houses in the way they expected. This made him seem odd. But he had so little in common with the Penang set, that he could in no circumstances have made real friends. His brother officials, however, had to admire his efficiency as assistant secretary. He could draft a despatch better than anyone else on the staff. When, as happened often, there was correspondence with the Malay nobles on the mainland, he could translate their letters and also reply in Malay. In fact, he made himself indispensable, developing rapidly into a first-class secretariat man. There was a great deal of work involved in setting the new Presidency on its feet. An arsenal and docks had to be constructed, teak imported from Burma for ship building, houses built, the town's amenities improved. So able did he show himself, so ready to accept responsibility, take on work which others could not manage, that in March 1807, eighteen months after his arrival, when the post of Chief Secretary to the Governor fell vacant, he was appointed, all such matters as administration, shipping, control of prices, discipline, having to pass under his eye. His salary was raised to £2,000 a year. Such promotion was meteoric. From being a clerk in Leadenhall Street on £70 a year, he had become at twenty-six the official head under the Governor in Council of the fourth Presidency.

First Days at Penang

He had managed, in spite of these secretarial labours, to push his studies of the Orient. It so happened that in October 1805 a certain Dr. John Leyden, a doctor in the medical establishment in Bengal, was sent to Penang to recuperate after an illness. Dr. Leyden, though only thirty, was a great oriental scholar, another example of precocity. Lord Minto, writing of him a few years later, has: 'Dr. Leyden's learning is stupendous . . . He has as intimate and profound a knowledge of the geography, history, mutual relations, religion, character and manners of every tribe in Asia, as he has of their language.' This, no doubt, is hyperbole, but there is no doubt that Leyden, who was the son of a Highland shepherd and at nineteen had taken honours at Edinburgh University in Hebrew, Arabic, Theology and Medicine, was another prodigy. His memory was phenomenal and his flow of talk unceasing, and was conducted, says Minto, 'in a shrill, piercing, and at the same time grating voice'. He sounds a sad bore, but for Raffles he was just the man he required to guide him in his studies. Raffles invited him to stay. He was somewhat of an invalid at the moment. Olivia Raffles nursed him back to health. By the end of a three months' visit he had become Raffles's close friend. Olivia seemed to him the most wonderful woman he had ever met, so clever, so kind, so beautiful. He worshipped her. Many of the letters he wrote to her afterwards are extant, as are some poems, for as in Thomas Moore's case, she inspired his muse. The letters are turgid and facetious, and the poems may be termed effusions. Nevertheless, it is clear that he was much in love with her. But Raffles was so fond of him and admired his scholarship so much that he took the romance as a compliment. For Olivia no doubt he was no more than a happy distraction. As it turned out, he was able on his return to Calcutta to make himself very useful to Raffles. The occasion arose after 1807

John Leyden

when Lord Minto became Governor General in India. Minto was the man who started Raffles on the career which made him famous, and Leyden first drew Minto's attention to Raffles.

Chapter Three

RAFFLES'S FIRST MEETING
WITH MINTO

*Arrival in India of Lord Minto as Governor General –
Napoleon's Oriental designs threaten the East India Company – Minto's character – The Marquess Wellesley's character – Minto first hears of Raffles and desires him to report
on East Asian affairs – Raffles goes to Calcutta to see Minto
– Raffles appointed his agent to advise on projected invasion
of Java, and goes to Malacca – description of Raffles by his
former servant, the seaman Edward Robarts*

Lord Minto reached Calcutta in July 1807. He had been
chairman of the Board of Control in London and so
knew a good deal about the East India Company's
affairs. Though the battle of Trafalgar in 1805 had ended any
immediate chance of Napoleon putting his vast oriental ambitions into practice by means of a naval expedition, his
victory at Austerlitz six weeks later, which made him master
of Europe at thirty-six, encouraged him to believe that he
could advance on India through Persia, after preparing the
way by agreements with the Afghans and the Mahrattas, two
formidably armed antagonists of the Company. Moreover,
he had bases at Mauritius and Bourbon, islands off the African
coast, whence his frigates could harass the Company's
merchantmen in the Indian Ocean on their way home via the

Cape, and bases, too, in Java, which, after he had annexed
Holland, became a French possession. He appointed a rene-
gade Dutchman, Daendels, to the command of that island,
which lying as it did on the flank of the Calcutta-Canton
trade route, was well situated to damage the Company. In
sum, Minto had succeeded to the Governor-Generalship at a
moment when the European situation was threatening. His
policy and, as it happened, Raffles's career were determined
by these events.

Minto, a Scottish nobleman, was a very different sort of
man from the Marquess Wellesley, his predecessor as Governor General, who by his military victories in India, when
his brother, the future Duke of Wellington, commanded an
army, had presented the Company with an empire, a present
which the Company declared they did not want and could
not afford. Minto's instructions were to economise, but faced
with the Napoleonic threat, he was obliged to forestall it. In
character he had much in common with Raffles, whom, of
course, he had never heard of when he landed in Calcutta.
He, too, was tender, a great family man; and interested in
the history and religions of the East. His sense of responsibility for the welfare of the native inhabitants was more
acute than that felt by his predecessors. He amusingly records
in a letter to his wife, written soon after his arrival, his dislike
of the ceremonial maintained at Government House. It was
less overwhelming than in the Marquess Wellesley's time,
who enjoyed that sort of thing, but it still remained far more
elaborate than Minto cared for. He writes: 'I drive out almost
every morning and evening. The formality of these airings is
uncomfortable to me to a degree that I cannot accustom
myself to. I am always followed by an officer and six troopers
of the bodyguard. This cannot be dispensed with. Four syces
or horse-keepers with fly flappers ran alongside the horses

until I positively rebelled against this annoyance. Everybody, Europeans and natives, salaams as I pass and the natives who swarm, draw up in lines and touch the ground almost with their heads.' Still worse was the palanquin in which he was sometimes carried. Thirty attendants formed a procession, carrying gold and silver maces, halberds, embroidered fans and cow tails to keep the flies off. 'All these run on foot at a round trot, some of them proclaiming my titles.' Even in the private rooms of Government House he was moidered by the attentions of his servants. 'These give you a regular military salute every time you stir out of your room, besides four or five with maces running before you.'

These citations predispose one to like Lord Minto, just as we are disposed to dislike Lord Curzon, who, though a viceroy of modern times, took seriously the adulations of the crowd and the deference of his subordinates as properly due to a superior person. The Marquess Wellesley, extravagantly flamboyant no doubt, is not displeasing in this sense because his dazzle had a joyous exuberance. It is true that his weakness for stage effects went very far. The diarist, Joseph Farington, under date 8 April 1811, records that when the Marquess sat to Sir Thomas Lawrence for his portrait, his lips were rouged, and Macaulay, after a visit to him at a later date, wrote: 'Such a blooming old swain I never saw: his hair combed with exquisite nicety, a waistcoat of driven snow, and a Star and Garter put on with rare skill.' But the great Duke's brother can be excused such foibles. They are mentioned only to show how very different a Governor General was Lord Minto. Nevertheless, modest though Minto was, as Governor General he was a splendid personage and notice by him spelt fortune. Raffles knew this very well; he knew that unless Minto took him up he would have to vegetate in the secretariat of Penang, lacking opportunity to rise to the height he felt capable of attaining. But to attract Lord Minto's attention was not to be quickly done; he was a very busy man, who for the first three years of office had his eyes fixed westward, the direction from which emanated the Napoleonic threat to India, which he sought to stem in Persia and Afghanistan by missions to the courts of their rulers. So from March 1807 when Raffles became Chief Secretary in Penang until July 1810 when at last he came face to face with Minto, he was tied to a routine, his office work so heavy that, as he declares in one of his letters, he feared his health would not stand the strain.

In 1810, Lord Minto, his eyes now turned south-east, began to consider how the French could be cleared out of Java. This was the sphere in which Raffles had become an expert. During two visits he had paid to Malacca, the former Dutch strong point in the Straits of that name, he foresaw that this area would shortly become the centre of interest and sought to acquire first-hand information about the posture of its affairs. He became personally acquainted with many of the Malay rulers, and inquired what was their attitude to Franco-Dutch rule in Java, which was oppressive, for Daendels, Napoleon's nominee, was a tyrant. He embodied his views on the whole situation in a lengthy report, which disclosed a statesman's grasp of the intricate pattern of South Asian politics. The report was submitted, as required, to his immediate superior, the Governor of Penang, who was neither competent nor inclined to rate it at its true value, for Raffles was too brilliant a man to be appreciated as a subordinate. But he had his friend Leyden at the Indian capital, and Leyden, when he had the chance, drew Minto's attention to him. In a letter written by Olivia to Leyden she refers to the complimentary way Minto mentioned Raffles on a public occasion and ascribes it to prompting by Leyden: 'Who but you could, who but your dear self would have remembered my beloved and in *every way worthy husband* in the elegant and honourable manner in which we saw his name' (in a published account of Minto's speech). She continues: 'Ah, my dear friend, . . . the little paltry wretches here (Penang) were astonished and nearly maddened by envy . . . They may bark as a dog does at the Moon and with as much effect.' A little later Leyden wrote to Raffles: 'I laid before Lord Minto . . . the m.s. concerning Malacca, with which he was greatly pleased, and desired me to say he should be grateful in receiving immediately from yourself any communications respecting the Eastern parts of a similar nature.'

This news and other hints that Lord Minto had a high opinion of his capacities and was reported to be even thinking of a post for him as Governor of the Moluccas, an outlying part of the Dutch East Indies, now controlled by the British, told Raffles that the moment had come for him to go and see the Governor General. Obtaining leave of absence from Penang, he embarked on a Malay proa, as no British ship was available, and he was too impatient to wait for one, and reached Calcutta at the end of June 1810. He had with him more notes about the Straits and Java which Leyden had told him Minto would be glad to read. A fortnight after his arrival he was received by him. 'I met with the kindest reception from Lord Minto,' he wrote to Olivia, who had remained in Penang, and described his first meeting with the man who afterwards became his firm friend. As the conversation proceeded, Minto perceived that Raffles was the very person he required to further his plans. On Raffles mentioning Java, 'his lordship', he says, 'cast a look of such scrutiny, anticipation and kindness upon me, as I shall never forget'. Raffles was only twenty-nine. His lordship, Governor General and surrounded by all the state of that great office, was in his sixtieth year. But the vast difference in age and rank between them was no obstacle to a warm understanding. Minto asked him to supply at once any information concerning Java he possessed. How strong was Daendels? Had he the backing of the Dutch residents in Java? Would the Javanese nobility, the princes or Regents as they were termed, support Daendels if Java was invaded by the British?

Questioned in this way, Raffles was able to give reassuring answers and suggested that Minto should appoint him his agent for Malaya with Malacca as his headquarters and authority to report, not through the Penang government, but direct to the Governor General. He would get secretly in touch with the Javanese Regents and ascertain how far they would co-operate. This was precisely what Minto wanted. It also was essential for him to have firsthand information about the right moment to launch the invasion and on what part of the coast the troops should be landed. He created for Raffles the post of Agent to the Governor General in Malaya. Raffles remained in Calcutta till 10 October on Minto's staff. Leyden was brought in to assist him.

In this sudden manner Raffles jumped over the head of the Penang government. With Java's conquest viewed as the project of the moment, Raffles, as the Governor General's trusted emissary for this great undertaking, had an appointment more important than the Governor of Penang's. One can well understand that this was not pleasant news when it reached Penang where the officials already felt that Raffles was too big for his boots. On 19 October he left Calcutta on his new assignment, the Honourable Company's brig *Ariel* being placed at his disposal. It was arranged that he should call at Penang *en route* for Malacca, there to pick up his family, sell his house and pack his belongings.

There exists a little glimpse of him in this very October

Raffles's First Meeting with Minto

1810 in *The Narrative of Edward Robarts*, never published in its entirety but quoted in Wurtzburg's *Raffles of the Eastern Isles* (1954). Robarts was a common sailor who after marrying one of the belles of Tahiti was for a while servant in Penang to Mrs Thomson, the sister whom Raffles brought out with him in 1805. On Thomson's death Robarts entered Raffles's employ, but left him to look for a better paid job in Calcutta some months before Raffles himself went there. This he failed to find and was in a poor way when in October 1810 he came across his former master. His *Narrative* has: 'As I was going through Tank Square Sir T. R. Raffles (Robarts in a touching way knights him six years before that event) passed me in a palenkeen. He looked at me but as it was raining very hard I did not stop as a great man is easy found when no one knows a poor one. Some few days afterwards I found out where Sir T.R. lived. When first I came to the house the first I saw was a Malay boy who was formerly servant to Mr Thompson. On seeing me the Boy ran up stairs to inform Sir T.R. that I was below. He ran half way downstairs to meet me; he received me with that friendly manner as tho' I was his equal. He conducted me to a room where the immortal Dr Leyden was sitting and introduced me to him.'

In the conversation which ensued Robarts told Raffles how, being out of a job, he employed his time in writing memoirs of all he had gone through since leaving London. 'What says he you have turned author, I replied anything to raise the wind for an honest morsel. He laughed. What says Dr L raise the wind? Yes Sir replied I – I have been lying becalmed these ten months and if a breeze does not spring up my unfortunate Bark will founder on the rocks of Adversity . . . Sir T.R. eagerly inquired about my family and wished to see them; a day was appointed. The day arrived, we went to Dr Ls house . . . On entering the room Sir T.R. met my wife, our past happy situation at Penang recalld to her mind she burst into tears and lent on his shoulder. He supported her kindly and conducted her to a chair . . . Dr L helpt my wife to a glass of wine, Sir T.R. then said to Dr L you will do me a personal kindness in helping Robarts to some employment . . . You may trust him with gold untold. Well replied Dr L I will see what I can do for him. Dr L then desired me to come every day to write my narrative. A room was appointed for me to write in. Sir T.R. being come on Publick duty he was mostly at Government house. He desired me to see him before his departure but the pressure of his duty debarred me that happiness.'

Such is the charming glimpse the seaman manages to evoke of the Agent Extraordinary of the Governor General, about to set out on the adventure which was to lead to the most exciting period of his life. The MS. of the unpublished *Narrative* is in the Advocates' Library, Edinburgh, and must be one of the few books in existence written by a sailor before the mast.

Leyden gave Raffles a letter for Olivia, painfully facetious as usual, which contains however this plain sentence: 'R's success here I regard as in every respect compleat. If he succeeds in his present objects, he will have a much finer game to play than he has hitherto had,' far better, he adds, than the rumoured Molucca appointment.

Chapter Four

THE JAVA EXPEDITION

Raffles at Penang en route for Malacca – Jealousy of officials there – Raffles described by Abdullah on his arrival at Malacca – Minto's disembarkation at Malacca described by Abdullah – Minto releases slaves – he gives a ball – is given an orang-outang – meets Olivia – Leyden on his staff as assistant to Raffles – Invasion of Java launched from Malacca

The *Ariel* anchored at Penang on 17 November 1810. Raffles had with him a letter from Minto to the Governor, Charles Bruce, brother of the Lord Elgin who bought the Parthenon metopes now in the British Museum. The letter authorized him to indent for such stores as he required and draw sufficient money to cover the expense of the new office in Malacca, without having to obtain the Governor in Council's sanction. As the nature of his employment was secret, Bruce was instructed not to divulge its object to his Council. That their late Chief Secretary had been taken up by Minto and given almost plenipotentiary powers was galling enough for the Penang councillors, who felt further slighted by being held unfit to hear precisely the nature of his employment. Raffles, however, was a man who never showed off. There was nothing of the upstart about his manner. He went quietly about his business, loaded the stores

required, drew the money, sold his house and departed for
Malacca after a stay of a fortnight, taking not only Olivia
with him but his widowed sister and two other sisters who
had recently come out from home in the hope of securing
husbands.

A description of Raffles's appearance at this time occurs
in the *Memoirs* of a certain Malay called Abdullah, a resident
of Malacca, who in 1810 was in his 'teens and became a clerk
in Raffles's office. Abdullah declares him to have been of
medium height, with a broad forehead, well-shaped head,
high nose, rather hollow cheeks and a slight stoop. 'He was
most courteous in his intercourse with all men. He had a
sweet expression on his face, was extremely affable and liberal,
and listened with attention when people spoke to him.' This
pleased the proud Malays, who in general found Europeans
very offensive. They were also astonished at his interest in
things Malay, their history, the botany of Malaya, its zoology.
He paid assistants out of his own pocket to collect moths,
insects, butterflies, others to collect plants, others coral, oyster
shells, fishes, others to buy Malay books. No European of this
sort had ever been seen before. His love of animals was a
revelation to Abdullah. The Malay Sultan of Sambar in
Borneo sent him an orang-outang. He dressed it in trousers, a
coat and hat and made a great pet of it. Abdullah had never
realised before how close animals were to humanity and came
to the conclusion that only the orang-outang's inability to
speak distinguished it from a man. But it understood human
language. 'When I was engaged in writing it would come
softly up to the table and slowly take my pen. When I said
to put it down, down it would put it.' Abdullah too has
something to say about how Raffles got on good terms with
the Malay Sultans and nobles by his pleasant manner and by
talking to them in their own language. And it was not only

with the upper class that he conversed; 'the poorest could speak to him.' Indeed, Abdullah's admiration overflows. 'If my experience be not at fault, there was not his equal in this world in skill or largeness of heart.'

Abdullah, who, as we shall see, was again in Raffles's employ later on, was perhaps his greatest fan.

These citations suggest that Raffles, though the Governor General's Agent on business of the first importance and urgency, found time to pursue the studies into Oriental lore which from the start had so much attracted him and were to contribute materially to his fame. He was indefatigable for every sort of knowledge.

Nevertheless, his business as Agent necessarily occupied most of his time and caused him, as Abdullah also noted, to sit up till 12.0 or 1.0 at night, reading and writing. He sent agents to Java to sound the Regents there, seek their support in advance. Would the Dutch go back on the French and come over when the British landed? A copious correspondence passed between him and Minto, whom he advised that a force of 3,000 European troops, 6,000 from the Company's sepoy army, 500 cavalry and a train of horse artillery would suffice for the conquest, though the French and Dutch forces were estimated at 14,000. He felt pretty sure, he said, that the Javanese Regents would come over. Finally he submitted that May 1811 should be the date, as the winds would then be most favourable.

By January 1811, a month or so after Raffles's arrival at Malacca, Minto was already making his first moves. He had decided to lead the expedition in person, entailing an absence from India of several months, an unprecedented course for a Governor General. The Board of Control in London had sanctioned the invasion. It had already sanctioned the assault on the French naval bases of Mauritius and Bourbon, which were captured early in the year 1811. The seas thus cleared of French warships, the expedition with its troop transports was under no threat. May was fixed for the fleet and transports to assemble in Malacca. 'I will meet you there,' Minto wrote, 'and with yourself the final plans, military and political, will be settled.' Thus Raffles was taken into Minto's inner councils. And he was promoted from Agent to be Secretary to the Governor General. In a letter of Minto's to his wife, dated 25 February 1811, he describes Raffles as 'a very clever, able, active and judicious man'.

Minto arrived at Malacca on 18 May 1811, where part of the naval and military forces of invasion had already assembled. The youthful Abdullah saw him land and, as he gives a more vivid account of the occasion than anyone else, he should be quoted. 'I guessed in my mind as to his appearance, position and height, that these would be great and his dress gorgeous, but his appearance was of one who was middle-aged, thin of body, had soft manners and a sweet countenance, and I felt that he could not carry 30 lbs so slow were his motions. His coat was black cloth, trousers the same. When the leading men desired to pay their respects, they remained at a distance, none daring to grasp his hand and they took off their hats and bowed their bodies.'

It is to be recalled that as Malacca was a Dutch settlement, originally Portuguese, which had come into British possession only sixteen years previously and been made a dependency of Penang, its upper class was Dutch and Malayo-Dutch, for the Portuguese remnant had by this time been largely absorbed by the Malays and Chinese. The head of the local government was the British Resident, William Farquhar, who had been there since 1796 and so had had nine years longer experience of the Straits than had Raffles, which made him envious of the latter's sudden elevation to be the Governor General's confidant and adviser. Later he was to give him some trouble, for he believed that Raffles had purloined his ideas without acknowledgement.

To continue Abdullah's amusing description. 'When His Lordship landed, he bowed to the right and left, then slowly walked up the centre between the files of soldiers, the cannon roaring all the time. He had not the remotest appearance of pomposity and lofty-headedness; there was a real modesty and kindness of expression. He returned the salutations of the poor.'

Minto made his way on foot to Government House, an old building of some architectural quality, built by the Portuguese but very stuffy, which lay on the stretch of flat near the anchorage. 'All the leading men of Malacca followed him, but of these Mr Raffles was the only one who dared approach close to him.'

After an interval Lord Minto set out on a tour of inspection. At the debtors' prison he found some who had been there as long as three years. 'All the prisoners came forward, some prostrating themselves before his feet, and others weeping.' The jailer tried to keep them back, but Minto was touched by their misery and conceiving that it was a cruelty to keep debtors indefinitely in jail, though even in England this was not unusual, he told the jailer to let them be and assured them that he would soon direct Mr Farquhar to release them.

Abdullah has something to say of what Minto did on the days following, especially of his inspection of the civil prison, a medieval type of building dating from the mid-sixteenth century, when the Portuguese first took Malacca from the Malays. It had a black hole of a dungeon, which the Dutch had continued to use, and Mr Farquhar had seen no reason to abolish, for his policy was to maintain the Dutch system of administration; his staff, in fact, was entirely Dutch. Three convicts were in the dark of the dungeon. Minto released them at once and directed that the dungeon be blocked up. He noticed also certain instruments of torture and ordered them to be destroyed. Abdullah enormously admired such humanity, a trait he held to be the mark of the really great man and which he had already observed that Raffles possessed.

In a further glimpse of Minto he says: 'On a certain evening Lord Minto took a walk as far as the residence of Mr Raffles to see the garden.' (Raffles had already collected a variety of interesting plants.) Minto was conducted by Raffles into the room where his clerks and assistants were working. 'We rose to pay our respects. And as he was passing near my desk, I retired as I was the smallest there and the youngest. On this His Lordship took me by the hand saying in the language of Hindustan: "Are you well?" I felt his hand that it was as soft as a child of one year old.' He advised Abdullah to learn English, which he set out to do before long.

Lord Minto in his sprightly letters to his wife (who never came out to India), has some further particulars on the Malacca visit which help us to understand why he and Raffles drew so close to each other. They were interested in the same things; their hearts were touched by the same things.

Three weeks after his arrival Minto gave a ball at Government House for the Dutch (most of whom were of mixed blood), the only section of the 15,000 inhabitants which was acquainted with such a western entertainment as a dance. The young women were all Eurasian, 'intensely and beautifully brown' says Minto, who much admired them and the

way they flirted. A few of the elderly women were pure
Dutch, colonial matrons old style. John Crawfurd, an E.I.
Company official, writing of a Government House ball in
Malacca ten years later, is here more explicit. 'Out of thirty-
seven ladies, two or three only were Europeans, and the rest
born in the country with a large admixture of Asiatic blood.
The female dress of the younger part was in English fashion;
and a very few only of the elderly ladies dressed in the Malay
loose gown or wore the hair in the Malay fashion.' As
these duennas watched the dancing they chewed betel and
used large brass spittoons. The Dutch mixed more with the
local inhabitants and met them on a greater social equality
than the English at this period and later, though Dutch
colonialism as an economic system was more oppressive than
the English variety.

Before the ball Minto did something quite extraordinary;
he released all the government's slaves, nineteen in number.
'I presented each with my own hand a certificate of their freedom and four dollars.' In 1807 British ships had been forbidden by law to carry slaves, but though the slave trade,
for the British, ended that year, the slaves actually in British
possessions were not emancipated until 1833. For Minto to
emancipate nineteen slaves in Malacca on 7 June 1811 was a
gesture characteristic of him and one which delighted Raffles.
Not that it altered the general state of slavery which prevailed.
There was a large trade in slaves carried on by the Malays
throughout the area. They were imported from the islands in
proas, those swift Malay sailers with sharp bow and stern. The
slavers, who were often pirates, captured them where they
could, especially from small unprotected villages near the
mouths of rivers. Outside the trade, a man might be reduced
to slavery for debt. Minto tells his wife: 'Men may gamble
their children, their wives and lastly themselves into slavery

in satisfaction of bets upon fighting cocks.' Cock fighting was
a sport the Malays were mad on. Minto then writes how he
himself had just become the master of several slaves. The
Sultan of Bali had sent him as a present five boys and two
girls. He emancipated them, of course, but was keeping them
on as servants; Raffles was taking one or two. He had one
slave more, he continued, presented to him by a Borneo
sultan. This was an orang-outang (the words are Malay for
wild man). But, says Minto, 'he is much too civilized to
deserve the name of wild. I saw him yesterday sitting on a
stool and eating his rice on a table like a Christian gentleman'.
So both Minto and Raffles had orang-outang pets.

As Olivia had not gone with her husband to Calcutta,
Minto met her for the first time in Malacca and tells his wife:
'Mrs Raffles is a great lady with dark eyes, lively manner,
accomplished and clever.' He was much taken with her,
thought her beautiful, and records the story, mentioned
earlier, that Thomas Moore had adored her. She was adored
again, for Leyden had arrived in Minto's suite. His romantic
passion, roused when he met her at Penang in 1805, fanned
by the letters and poems they had exchanged since then, was
still as strong as ever. Minto had brought him as additional
adviser and made him Raffles's assistant. His 'learning is
stupendous' he writes at this time, but though he admired
his erudition he found him exhausting to talk to, because he
would run off the point. 'I have often', he wrote, 'tried to fix
him to the point in hand, and the only way has been a more
peremptory call than I like to use to one whom I esteem so
highly.' But Raffles had no reservations. His friendship for
Leyden was the warmest he ever formed. He had not the
smallest objection to his romantic attachment to Olivia. In
1811 Leyden was thirty-six, Olivia forty. Their association
now was very brief. Minto with his staff, with Leyden,

The Java Expedition

Raffles and the rest, the troops and warships, left for Java on 18 June 1811, exactly a month after his arrival. Leyden and Olivia were never to meet again. His death was only nine weeks distant.

Chapter Five

CONQUEST OF JAVA

Besides his diplomatic approaches to the Regents of Java and the Sultans of other islands, Raffles had undertaken the task of working out the best route for the invasion fleet to follow, a duty for which the Navy would normally have been responsible. But the navigating officers had only a scanty knowledge of the waters between Malacca and Java. The charts were incorrect, not all the small islands and but few of the shoals were marked. The Dutch had never been communicative on such matters, as they wanted no trespassers in their spice-island preserves. The direction, too, of the wind was a problem. Could one sail from Malacca to Java in the month of June? They should have got off in May. The distance in a straight line was not great. From Malacca to the eastern exit of the Straits was some 150 miles; from there south-east to Java another 500 miles, say 650 miles altogether. But sailing ships do not go in a straight line. Information

collected by Raffles revealed that in June, with winds the way
they were, the route from the mouth of the Straits would
have to be N.E. to the north point of Borneo, a distance of
over 1,000 miles, and thence down the west coast of Borneo
and across the strait dividing it from Java, another 1,300 miles,
altogether 2,450 instead of 650 miles. Naval experts, though
inclined at first to disagree and suggest a route east of Borneo,
finally adopted Raffles's suggestion. The voyage was going
to take some weeks, but the chances were that the fleet and
transports would arrive without mishap.

In fact, the voyage lasted from 11 June 1811 to the first
week in August, a matter of six weeks. Raffles was on the
frigate *Modeste* with Minto and Leyden. The fleet, consisting
of some ninety sail, was slow and the *Modeste*, which started
a few days later than the main body, caught up and was the
first to arrive in Javanese waters. On the way they passed
Singapore, a swampy thinly populated island belonging to
the Sultanate of Johore. The battle of Waterloo was still four
years away. The peace settlement and the restoration of the
Dutch, freed from French domination, to a key position in
the European balance of power, was still further in the future.
That the settlement would entail the founding of a new
British strong point in the Straits of Malacca had crossed
nobody's mind. Nevertheless, Raffles's passage in the *Modeste*
within cannonshot of Singapore has thematic point. It was
his first view of the island destined in a few years to be so
closely associated with his fame.

After passing Singapore, the fleet threaded its way between
the nearby archipelagoes of Rhio and Linga, and steering
N.E. came to Borneo's most northerly spot, Balambangan
island, at whose lovely south-sea beach anchor was cast,
water taken on and the sick put ashore to recuperate.

By 4 August 1811 the whole fleet was lying off Batavia,

the capital of Java, not a vessel, a man or even a spar having been lost *en route*. Raffles was excited by so successful a landfall, to which his advice had contributed so much. He wrote to Ramsay, his old friend of East India House days: 'You always said I was a strange wild fellow, insatiable in ambition,' and declared the moment the most inspiring so far in his life. 'I am as happy as it is possible for a man to be.' And to his cousin, Dr Raffles, he wrote of the arrival: 'I will not attempt to say what my feelings were on the occasion.' And he added, what no doubt contributed to his high spirits, that Lord Minto had promised him the governorship of Java, if the expedition were successful.

The troops were landed without opposition some ten miles east of Batavia. To impress on the population that the British were deliverers from the French and not conquerors, proclamations to that effect were circulated among the native inhabitants and the Dutch were abjured to abandon France. The British and sepoy soldiers had strict orders to harm nobody, not to molest villagers or loot their property, orders which they obeyed to the surprise of all. A Dutchman, Janssens by name, had succeeded Daendels to the command of the Javanese forces. As he was uncertain of the loyalty of his men, he withdrew his army to the shelter of a fortress called Cornelis six miles inland. Batavia, left without defenders, surrendered at once and the invaders moved on Cornelis on 10 August. When the artillery came up, the walls were breached and, led by a dashing Irishman, Colonel Gillespie, the troops rushed in. Cornelis was taken, Janssens's men killed or captured. He fled with a remnant of six hundred eastwards to Samarang. When the Dutch troops saw that the battle was going against them, they flung their French cockades in the mud and trampled on them. The rout was complete.

On 29 August, only twenty-five days after the landing, Minto issued a proclamation declaring Franco-Dutch sovereignty at an end and Java annexed by the East India Company. It was one of the shortest campaigns on record. Napoleon, as had been rightly anticipated, had been unable to protect his eastern possessions. With Mauritius gone and Java taken he had now no foothold in Asia. No matter how he came out of the struggle in Europe, India and the trade route to China via the Straits of Malacca were secure for the foreseeable future.

The East India Company's view had been against annexation because it feared that Java, potentially rich though it was, would turn out in practice a liability. The idea had been to leave the island in the hands of the Regents. Java without the French was no threat to India or the trade. Minto, however, regarded annexation as essential. If the British withdrew, anarchy would result and a massacre of the Dutch and half Dutch population would probably follow, as the Javanese hated the Dutch. He therefore took the responsibility of setting up a British administration. His decision to appoint Raffles, young though he was, to the head of it, had been taken on the ground that he was eminently fitted for the appointment. The success of the invasion had been assured by the thoroughness of his preliminary inquiries and the valuable information he had gathered about the opposition likely to be met. He had done more than any other man to plan the invasion. Minto also felt that he had just the right character; his inclination would be to govern Java in the interests of the Javanese, a liberal policy for which Minto stood. So, on 11 September he was appointed Lieutenant-Governor. His Council consisted of three members, one of whom was Colonel Gillespie, who had distinguished himself so much in the fighting. He was to command the garrison to be left in

Java. Minto himself would withdraw in October with the main body of the invasion force.

The day before Minto issued his proclamation annexing Java, Leyden died. He had been given the duty of inspecting the Dutch archives kept in the secretariat in Batavia. It was cooler in the stone vaults where the records were stored than in the heat outdoors. The sudden change of temperature proved fatal. Leyden had a slight fever when he went into the vaults. He was over-tired too, and generally run down. Absorbed in what was for him a very interesting piece of work, he stayed some time, got chilled and when he left the store-room his fever was much worse. A violent attack of malaria had come on. When Raffles was informed, he hastened to his friend's side and found him unconscious. 'I attended him from first to last,' he wrote. Leyden died next day. His death was an irreparable loss for Raffles, who not only was very fond of him but had planned to make him his principal secretary and looked forward 'to the happiness of having, as an inmate of my family, one with whom I could take counsel both in public and in private; whose judgment would aid and whose affection would cheer in the responsible position I was about to undertake'. In this sentence we see a reflection of Olivia's grief. Leyden's death, indeed, was a calamity. No one could take his place, there was no one with anything approaching his expert knowledge. The capture of Java opened a vast field for research. Only Leyden could have taken full advantage of the opportunity. 'We have lost in him a host of men,' Raffles wrote to Marsden, the historian of Sumatra. 'Eastern literature has lost in him its firmest support.' Raffles felt that he faced the tasks of the future alone, though he had Minto's support.

But Minto would be leaving Java in six weeks. Moreover, Minto's position was not secure. He knew quite well that

London – the Court of Directors and the Board of Control – was unlikely to be impressed by the Java *coup*. They had sanctioned the invasion and the driving out of the French, but had not yet sanctioned the annexation nor the appointment of Raffles as Lieutenant-Governor of what amounted to a fifth Presidency, for Raffles was to report to, and take his orders from, the Governor General in Council. Minto's case was that the British had made themselves, by their action of taking the island, responsible for its administration, a task which would redound to their credit and also enhance their power. With the other islands of the former Dutch domain – Sumatra, Bali, the Moluccas, Borneo, to mention only the most important – he had added to India a new empire of the eastern seas, an empire potentially very rich and which, together with India, would give England, the little island of the west, dominion through sea power over all Asia. But, said his critics on the Court and the Board, this is far beyond any ambition we have ever entertained, or any instruction sent to you. During all our management of the Company's affairs we have set our faces against annexation of new territories. It is true that in India we have annexed large areas and organized their administration. We were forced to do this in order to safeguard what we already possessed. For a company, whose *raison d'être* is wholly commercial, it was a speculation, which often did not pay. The administration of Java, they went on, was bound to be very expensive. The island's commerce had been largely disrupted as a result of the Napoleonic wars. There had been a blockade, the export trade was crippled. Before trade could be restored years would pass; the commercial system required overhaul from top to bottom. The Company would have to advance huge sums before profits began to come in. And all this at a time when England was engaged in Europe in a life and death struggle, which entailed financing allies and putting armies into Spain where the Peninsular war was in progress.

England herself was in a deplorable state of unrest. Prices had risen, the price of bread had doubled. There were riots everywhere. The Prince Regent was now hated in many quarters. He had become so lazy that he would not even sign his name on pending papers, or so Lady Minto wrote out to her husband. 'He gets up at 3 p.m.,' she declares. 'Before dressing he sees his jewellers, his tailors and his tradesmen.' Then dressing in a leisurely manner he went to Hertford House and got drunk. The public was gravely disturbed. The Prime Minister, Percival, was shot to the extravagant delight of the mob. Handbills were distributed offering £10,000 for the murder of the Regent.

This was no moment to add to burdens almost too heavy to bear. The taking of Java was not a stroke that could stay Napoleon's hand in Europe. The money already spent on the Java expedition and to be spent on the island's administration was far more urgently needed at home.

And these critics of Minto had a final argument: it was by no means certain that England would be able to retain Java and its dependencies when peace came. One hoped and believed that Napoleon would finally be defeated, for the countries in Europe, which he had overrun in his wild ambition to be Lord of the World, would at last unite against him.

When the peace settlement came, Holland would have to be built up again as a European power, a power which, adjacent to England, it was essential to have in close alliance. But Holland was ruined. It could not be restored to prosperity unless it got back its rich island empire. If such a restitution was likely – and even Minto feared it might be – what was the use of spending effort and money on somebody else's property? In sum, the annexation of Java was no better than a pig in a poke.

There were others, however, to remind the public that Napoleon was not yet defeated. Indeed, he was master of the West, the most powerful European, after the Caesars, who had ever existed. Rumour had it already that he intended a great stroke against Russia, which lay in the way of his vast ambitions. In 1812, less than a year after the taking of Java, he is stated to have declared to one of his marshals as his army stood poised on the Niemen: 'Suppose Moscow taken, Russia crushed, would it not be possible for a great French army to attain the Ganges? Once touched by the French sword, the scaffolding of mercantile India would fall to the ground.' And he said: 'I must now from the extremity of Europe invade Asia in order to take England.' In such circumstances was it not prudent to remain in occupation of Java and make it the bastion of British naval power in the Far East, from which counter-attacks against Napoleon could be mounted, should he penetrate as far as India?

Such was the fluidity of opinion in October 1811 when Minto bade Raffles farewell. Though he believed that what he had done was for the best and would be to the advantage of both England and Java, he did not expect to be praised or rewarded until justified by events, for he admits that he has 'deviated materially from instructions'. Indeed, he does not want reward, but only public acknowledgement of his services. His greatest solace is in the feeling that he has done right. If he has laid the foundation for a government in Java, better than the oppressive system obtaining before, 'I shall bear the want of rewards with the greatest equanimity and indifference' he tells his wife. He will be blessed by Java's five million inhabitants. In the same letter (3 October 1811) he informs her that he has almost finished the twenty volumes of Cicero which have been his leisure reading since he left Calcutta. He draws her attention particularly, in the original Latin, to the *Somnium Scipionis*, where the Roman declares virtue to be its own reward. 'I have become a great philosopher of late.' He feels sure that, when all the facts are known, what he has done on his own responsibility will be approved in London.

Minto left for India on 19 October 1811. On the 18th he dined alone with Raffles. They had a final discussion on the problems of the future. Raffles had been given wide reserve powers. While he was to be guided by his Council, consisting of Colonel Gillespie and two experienced Dutch civil servants, who had agreed to support a reformed administration and use all their influence to obtain the co-operation of the Dutch inhabitants, he was not bound to take their advice. His own decision on all matters was final, though if he differed from the Council he had to record his reasons and report to London. It was explicitly laid down that the military was subject to the civil power. There had been some pressure on Minto to make it a military government under a Commander-in-Chief. But, of course, this was quite out of the question since Minto was set on a benevolent policy of reform. Gillespie had received his appointment on the Council because of his gallantry at the battle of Cornelis, where he led the storm, though suffering from fever, and where he received a serious wound. Nevertheless, the Duke of Wellington's famous remark when Sir William Erskine was foisted on him by the Horse Guards applies here: 'There is nothing on earth so stupid as a "gallant officer".' Gillespie's stupidity was inability to grasp that as subordinate to the civil government he must obey its orders. He could not, moreover, distinguish foolhardiness from bravery; his gallantry was more often rashness. He had not grown up, though he was forty-five at

Conquest of Java

this time. To these faults of character was added a strain of malice, a defect which sat very ill on a person who prided himself on being an Irish gentleman. Minto was anxious to give Raffles every possible help, but did him a great disservice by appointing Gillespie commander of the forces and member of council, as will appear in the sequel.

He also misled Raffles in a point of financial importance or, perhaps it should be said, he accepted as sound Raffles's estimate of the economic situation in Java, a far too optimistic estimate which he, thirty years older and with his former experience as chairman of the Board of Control in London, should have seen to be so. Instead he endorsed Raffles's optimism in the strongest terms when writing home, and so committed him to undertaking that the administration of Java could be made to pay for itself.

These two matters, Gillespie's appointment and the understanding that Java would be no expense to the East India Company, gravely embarrassed Raffles later on, when Minto was not there to stand by him. After 19 October 1811 he was never to see his great patron and protector again, for two and a half years later he died, leaving Raffles alone to implement the promises they had made together.

Chapter Six

RAFFLES AS
LIEUTENANT-GOVERNOR OF JAVA

Reflections on Raffles's administration of Java – His resi-
dence at Buitenzorg – his entertainments – Olivia as hostess
– Raffles and Javanese Regents – His visit to the Sultan
of Solo – meets Dr Horsfield – thence to Jokyakarta – scene
in the Sultan's palace – agreement – Sultan breaks agreement
– Raffles marches against him with Gillespie – Sultan's
defeat – Conquest of Java now complete

Raffles's rule in Java lasted from September 1811 to
March 1816, four and a half years. He came to it after
serving without a break in the East for six years. In
modern times members of the Indian Civil Service were able
to spend six months or more in Europe every three years to
renew their health and energy. That Raffles had not this
advantage and that in his time the causes and cure of oriental
diseases had been little investigated, account for the ill health
from which he now began to suffer. Many of his colleagues
died, women and children were frequently carried off. That
he survived, though apparently not a man of robust constitution, is the more remarkable since he never spared himself.
His official labours were very heavy, his private studies in
Malayan history, life, religion, art, language – the whole unexplored oriental background of South East Asia – were

relentlessly pushed on. He survived, though he undermined his health; yet his enthusiasm, his emotional drive, his conviction that he was engaged on what was right and should be done urgently, bore him up, and illnesses, pain, exhaustion and every kind of aggravation did not suffice to discourage or stop him, for he was a man of indomitable spirit. His very optimism, his faith that all would come out well, was the cause of some of his troubles. But it was justified in the end. I think it can be said that everything he thought and did has been endorsed by opinion in the nineteenth and twentieth centuries.

His administration of Java, though it gave him for one reason and another a certain celebrity in England when he returned there in 1816, was not what made him the figure he was to become. His elevation into a protagonist on the world scene was due to one great stroke. Just as in 1757 the few hours in Plassey grove turned Clive, a minor East India Company officer, who afterwards did nothing in particular and went off his head, into the founder of the Indian Empire, so Raffles's stroke at Singapore, the Lion City, in 1819, embalmed him forever as a man who moulded the course of history in East Asia. His governorship of Java cannot be said to have led to his capital achievement except in so far as it instructed him how to bring it about. His administration is interesting, but for reasons only bordering the central drama of his life. A great deal of information survives on what he did during the four and a half years. It has tempted previous biographers to devote much space to describing what Java was like in 1811, what were the main features of Dutch life there, their economic policy, the condition of the Javanese and the state of their nobility, and the new procedures which Raffles inaugurated. Something of all this must be set out, but too much of it would bury Raffles under a mass of debris, as has happened to many remarkable men whose impact on their period has been obscured rather than illuminated by over-industrious biographers.

As soon as Olivia and his household arrived from Malacca, Raffles went to live at Buitenzorg, the country house of the former Dutch Governor General, Janssens, a palatial residence forty miles south of Batavia. It stood on higher ground than the capital and was away from the mosquito swamps of the coastal belt. The surroundings were picturesque. Torrents tumbled past the house and mountains stood up behind it. In this delightful spot Raffles did his entertaining and most of his official work, visiting Batavia only for short stays when special business required. His salary as Lieutenant Governor enabled him to entertain on the large scale he considered necessary if he were to get on friendly terms with the Dutch and with the Javanese notabilities. In fact, he enjoyed entertaining, as he was naturally gay in society. His manner made him appear pleased and warm whoever he was speaking to. Olivia was a great help, exactly the right kind of hostess for Java. She looked the part of first lady and yet knew how to mix. Dutch society, as in Malacca, was almost entirely Eurasian; the British officers and their wives tended to be stiff. But Olivia had the knack of making that sort of party go. Compared with the elegancies of Government House, Calcutta, the behaviour and appearance of the Dutch at Government House, Buitenzorg, were grotesque. Even Minto, at a ball given before he left, found the sight of his guests so queer that, though a man with few prejudices, he viewed the scene with some distaste. 'The whole colonial sex runs naturally to fat, partly from overfeeding and partly from want of exercise,' he wrote to his wife. The older Dutch ladies were of immense size and very ugly. The younger women were totally uneducated. Nevertheless, their animation and abandon in the waltz attracted him. And he called the British officers boobies for not letting themselves go and enjoying their embraces. Olivia, it seems, knew exactly how to handle them. And Raffles's natural inclination was to like everybody without distinction.

Besides winning over the Dutch, Raffles had to make sure of the loyalty of the Javanese Regents, the feudal lords whose former powers had been reduced by the Dutch but who remained proud and recalcitrant at heart. When Minto sent back to India 10,000 of the invading force of 15,000, some of these lords saw an opportunity to make themselves independent. The most important were the Sultans of Solo and Jokyakarta. Raffles sent John Crawfurd, the ablest and most intelligent of his staff, to the court of Jokyakarta as Resident, with a salary of £1,800 a year. He was to live on this salary and set an example of incorruptibility by not following the custom of the former Dutch Residents who took a percentage from opium sales and the sale of the aphrodisiac, birds'-nests. It is unnecessary here to unravel at length the complexities of the internal situation. Suffice it to say that Raffles decided to pay the Sultan of Jokyakarta a visit in December 1811, two months after Minto's departure, and try to reach an understanding with him. Jokyakarta is some 250 miles east of Batavia and near the south coast of the island. What follows are a few extracts from Raffles's letters to Minto and from the *Memoir* by his second wife published in 1830. These reflect the colour of the Javanese courts, indeed of all the courts of the Malay rulers whether on the mainland or on the islands. In our time Joseph Conrad has made us familiar with their atmosphere of ferocity, intrigue, pride and fanaticism.

En route for Jokyakarta Raffles visited the Sultan of Solo with whom he came to an amicable agreement, whereby the Sultan became a feudatory of the British government, was guaranteed protection and a fixed revenue. In token of his friendship he presented Raffles with an ancestral kris, a magical weapon of the utmost sanctity in the eyes of the donor, in short the most valuable antique he possessed. In this area Raffles came across Dr Horsfield, an American naturalist, antiquarian and artist, who had been in Java for eleven years in the employ of the Dutch. Raffles recognized him at once as a valuable assistant who could replace, to some extent, the lamented Leyden. He encouraged him by his immediate interest in his papers, maps and drawings, provided him with a salary and urged him to extend his studies in further direc-tions. Horsfield writes that this first meeting took place in the Sultan's hall of state. 'He came up to me and, with an affability and suavity of manner peculiar to himself, offered me his acquaintance without the formality of an introduc-tion.' From being a minor official, Horsfield became the Lieutenant Governor's collaborator and friend, one of several keen naturalists and archaeologists whom Raffles gathered round him and who by their notes, collections and explora-tions enabled him to write before he left his monumental *History of Java*, which William Daniell illustrated in a series of beautiful colour prints.

Having settled affairs in Solo, Raffles continued his journey to Jokyakarta, accompanied by a troop of dragoons and a detachment of Bengal sepoys, a force numbering about 900, for the Sultan, who had fallen out with Crawfurd, might, it was thought, prove dangerous.

His capital was a strongly fortified position three miles in circumference, surrounded by a moat and a stone wall forty-five feet high. The palace was in the centre among courtyards and the houses of the nobility. Passing through the north gate and over a large square bordered with trees, Raffles with his escort entered the huge hall of audience where the Sultan awaited him, surrounded by his lords and their armed retainers, some hundreds in number. Raffles noticed at once that the seating arrangements were such that if he took the place assigned to him he would be made to appear the Sultan's inferior or a petitioner for his favour. The expression on the Sultan's face was insolent. He did not rise to receive the head of the government. An alarming tension was in the air. Members of the Sultan's immediate suite were handling their kris as if about to draw them. Had Raffles walked into a trap? Were he and his escort about to be set upon and despatched by a fanatical rush of Malays, who seemed to be working up into a frenzy? The Sultan watched to see what his visitor would do. It was generally surmised afterwards that had Raffles shown any sign of fear and sat in the place put for him, the Sultan would have thought it safe to murder him and have given the signal which his people expected. But Raffles had the presence of mind to assert his authority in calm firm words. He would not sit down, he said, until the chairs were rearranged in a proper manner. His coolness, his confidence that he would be obeyed, sufficed. The Sultan ordered this to be done. Raffles sat down. Unperturbed, dignified and as if unaware that anything more than a trifling misunderstanding had arisen, he opened the proceedings, informing the Sultan of the agreement made by the Sultan of Solo and inviting him in a reasonable tone to do likewise. A discussion followed, and the Sultan made terms, considered adequate for the moment.

Some months later, however, he thought he saw an opportunity of resorting to his original design of driving the English out of Java and asserting the independence of that country. The greater part of the remaining British forces had been sent across the Straits of Sunda into the island of Sumatra to chastise a sultan there who had massacred the Dutch residents. Raffles was left with hardly a thousand men. He did not delay, however, when informed of what was brewing, and took the road to Jokyakarta. This time he had Gillespie with him. On the evening of 17 June 1812 they arrived outside the fortress and sent an ultimatum to the Sultan. But he, relying on the weakness of Raffles's forces and the strength of his fortifications, dismissed the messenger without an answer. Later, writing to Minto, Raffles reported: 'On the 18th June, in the afternoon, we commenced a heavy cannonade.' The Sultan, however, refused to parley, as the balls had not breached his wall. Gillespie now ordered a storm. It suited his temperament. He felt at home leading a ferocious hand to hand. The palace was carried after three hours' hard fighting. There were few casualties on the British side, but great slaughter on the other. Gillespie, however, who had been characteristically rash, received a deep wound in the left arm. 'Gillespie was himself' was the phrase Raffles used in his despatch. He went on to assure Minto that the conquest of Java was now complete. Hitherto the British held only the coast provinces. 'Never till this event could we call ourselves masters of the more valuable provinces of the interior . . . The European power is for the first time paramount in Java.' Minto replied in a private letter, praising Raffles's management of the affair and declared it 'very glorious to your administration. Nothing could be more excellent than all your arrangements'. He signs himself 'most truly and affectionately yours'. He had good reason to be pleased that his young protégé had done so well. Had Raffles made a mess of things, it would have been very difficult for Minto to have kept the Court and Board happy about the Java business, which from the first they had viewed with disquiet.

As it was, all seemed set fair for Raffles. But from this point his troubles began.

Chapter Seven

RAFFLES'S HUMANE POLICY

*Raffles sets out to reform existing Dutch methods of admini-
stration – Mercantilism superseded – Sale of government
lands to obtain silver to back paper currency – Raffles bids
at the auction – Minto shortly to leave India – Difficulties
with Gillespie – Gillespie recalled by Minto – scene at his
departure to new command in India*

During 1812 Raffles faced the problem of how to
transform the administration of Java. 'Let us do all
the good we can while we are here' was Minto's
last word before he left. Dutch administration was mercantile, a system very different from one designed to benefit
the native population. In the mercantile economic theory
matters were so arranged that the Dutch East India Company
bought all the country's products at a low figure, exported
them for sale to Holland where, having a monopoly, it could
get a profit of hundreds per cent. The peasants were forced
to grow only what they were ordered to grow, and were not
allowed to sell to anyone outside the Dutch Company. Im-
ports were restricted to a minimum on the theory that they
represented a loss to the Company. The British had applied
mercantilism to the American colonies, and it was against
mercantilism that they revolted. By 1812 mercantilism in
English eyes was a discredited system, oppressive and also

economically unsound. Minto and Raffles pitied the Javanese peasantry, forced to take a miserable price for their crop, taxed on that price, forced to labour on roads and public works without wages and in addition exposed to the caprices of the Regents, who as agents of the Company had the duty of seeing that the cultivator did his work as laid down, and who had the power to punish him and also make further exactions. The Javanese peasant was no better than a serf.

The administration of the British East India Company, founded on Mogul precedents, was in comparison much more liberal. The Indian cultivator owned or leased his land, could grow what crops he liked, sold in the general market, got the current price, and could appeal to properly constituted courts of law against injustice. He was not conscripted to do forced labour. He was taxed on the value of his outturn, estimated in advance after careful inquiry, the tax being collected directly from him by officials. A salaried bureaucracy existed, whose duty it was to see that he had fair play. Minto and Raffles planned to rescue the Javanese peasant by substituting this system for the mercantile. Clearly such a change could not be effected in a moment. A mass of new regulations had to be drawn up and a new bureaucracy trained to give effect to them. The Court of Directors had been assured that the change-over could be quickly effected and that the revenue, calculated on the new basis of a fair valuation of every acre in the great island, would soon come in. But this did not, could not, happen at once. Not enough money was collected to pay for the government, its troops, stores, etc. The deficit had to be met by grants from Indian revenues. The Court and the Board did not take kindly this failure to make ends meet. The situation was further complicated by the currency situation. The Dutch had used a paper currency which was now worthless as it was not backed with silver. To get silver to back it meant further borrowing from India. In November 1812 Raffles thought of a way to raise cash by auctioning government land. So that buyers might be sure that the auctions were *bona fide*, he led the way by buying some land for himself, even encouraging people to bid against him so as to obtain for government a good price.

In all this Minto continued to give Raffles the fullest support.

But Raffles's situation was not as strong as it looked. In July 1812 he was thirty-one years of age. He was drawing a salary of £8,000 a year. He was the ruler under the Governor General, his affectionate friend, of the Dutch empire consisting of Java, Sumatra, the Celebes, the Moluccas, Borneo and a host of lesser islands, lands potentially very rich, of vast extent, sitting on the South Seas, the link between India and the Far East. But his patron, his protector, the man who shared his views, a liberal like himself, a humanist, a scholar, was about to leave India. Minto's time was up as Governor General by the end of 1814. By then he would have held office for more than seven years. He had neither the health nor the desire to remain longer. Nor, as will appear, the option. When he went, unless his successor was to be as staunch a supporter, Raffles would stand alone. The unpleasant fact, as he knew very well, was that the Directors and the Board had become more critical of his ideas and achievements when it was clear that Java was not paying its way. Why should the East India Company have to bestow, at great expense, a new government on the Javanese people? The company wished them no harm. But after all it was a commercial not a charitable concern. Java did not pay. Worse, it was a liability. If the Dutch empire was to remain under British rule, the money expended now would, no doubt, be sound investment. But as everyone knew, the chances were that at the peace Britain would find it politically expedient to restore Holland's overseas possessions. That being so, Minto and Raffles's endeavours in Java were not business. It was nice to think that the Javanese were being treated well, but why should the East India Company have to foot the bill? Such were some of the uncertainties of Raffles's situation. Had he any security for the future?

In the early part of 1813 he was faced with an unpleasantness from another quarter. Hitherto he had been able to get on reasonably well with Gillespie, the commander of the forces and the senior member of his Council. But now a serious difference of opinion arose. After the recalcitrant Regents of Solo and Jokyakarta had been brought to heel, internal security was no longer threatened. British sovereignty was accepted by all. Under pressure to reduce the expense of his establishment, Raffles thought an economy might be affected by sending back to India the British regiments and replacing them by Sepoys, who were much cheaper. Gillespie opposed this view. He argued that Napoleon was still at large and that a French attempt to retake Java might occur at any time. Raffles was convinced that no such danger existed, though the news of Napoleon's disastrous campaign in Russia had not yet reached Java. Gillespie, extremely jealous about any matter touching his command, could not be brought to see the commonsense of Raffles's proposal. He had taken an increasingly melodramatic view of himself. Admirers who called him a hero, citing the dauntless manner in which he led the storms of Cornelis and Jokyakarta, encouraged him to assert himself. He seems to have thought that Raffles's appointment as Lieutenant-Governor might not be confirmed by London and that there was a chance Java would be handed over to military authority, with himself as military Governor. This led to his assuming an attitude towards Raffles which made it extremely difficult to deal with him in the daily course of business. He put forward the claim, for instance, that the finances of the army should not be subject to civil audit. He should be free to make what contracts and indents he liked, the bills to be paid by the government without check, a first step towards making the military independent. Raffles reported his eccentricities to Minto, who replied that the supremacy of the civil government must be maintained and that he agreed that the army might suitably be reduced.

During 1813 it became increasingly difficult to work with Gillespie, and Minto, on Raffles representing the matter, decided to recall him to a command in India. Before this happened, however, Gillespie seems to have tried to accommodate himself. On 23 September 1813 Raffles wrote to London: 'The difference with the Commander of the Forces, to which I was reluctantly compelled to allude in my last despatches, no longer exists.' Gillespie had admitted that Raffles was right about the relationship of the civil and military spheres. At the moment 'the measures of Government are conducted with perfect union and cordiality'. On 11 October 1813 Gillespie left Java for Calcutta on board a warship to take up his new command in India. He was seen off as far as the beach by Captain Thomas Travers, Raffles's secretary and friend, who kept a diary which is a reliable source. A man called Robinson, described by Travers as 'Raffles's most confidential friend', followed Gillespie on board to say farewell 'and had a long talk with him on deck, when Gillespie declared his attachment to Raffles and his positive determination to support every measure of his administration'. Robinson reported this to Raffles on coming ashore. But Gillespie had so volatile a character that assurances of friendship were worth little. He had, moreover, as has been hinted, a degree of malice in his nature. Raffles had got the better of him. It was he, not Raffles, who had to leave Java. One could not be sure what he would do when he got to Calcutta, particularly as Minto would have handed over the Governor Generalship to his successor, Lord Moira (afterwards the Marquess of Hastings), before Gillespie arrived. But Raffles's nature was not to be suspicious. He tended to believe a man's word. What Gillespie did came as a great surprise.

Chapter Eight

RAFFLES AND GILLESPIE

*During the voyage to Calcutta Gillespie, at the instance of a
dismissed official, Charles Blagrave, resolves to bring
charges against Raffles – Lord Minto hands over to Lord
Moira and leaves for England – Gillespie denounces Raffles
to Lord Moira – before leaving, Minto arranges reversion of
Bencoolen for Raffles when his appointment in Java at an
end – Gillespie's charges sent to Raffles for his explanation –
Raffles writes his reply – sends copy to London – Death of
Minto in England – Death of Olivia – Death of Gillespie*

Raffles hitherto had been a lucky man in the main, but
was now beset by an unlucky turn, which assumed of
a sudden such grave proportions as to threaten his
ruin.

We beheld Gillespie sailing off to Calcutta on 8 October
1813, apparently glad to be going to a new command and
on almost emotionally good terms with Raffles, for when he
bade Travers, Raffles's great admirer and intimate, goodbye on the beach, Travers records in his *Diary* that he himself
was in 'floods of tears' and that Gillespie 'took me by both
hands and swore eternal friendship'. At the moment Gillespie
evidently looked back on his two years in Java as a very
happy period. It was exciting to be a hero; he had had a good
time with the girls; been promoted Major-General. Differ-

ences there had been, but they were forgotten the day a few months back when he opened a ball by dancing with Olivia. Nevertheless, suddenly and unexpectedly he was to turn on Raffles. On board his ship was a certain Charles Blagrave, whom Raffles had appointed one of his secretaries in 1811, but had dismissed in March 1813 for some dishonesty or peculation. He had ordered him to take up a job in the Moluccas, but he booked a passage on Gillespie's ship going in the opposite direction. He now saw his chance of revenging himself on Raffles for his dismissal. During the two months' voyage he would work on the excitable, unstable Major-General.

The line he took was to tell Gillespie that as secretary things had come to his knowledge of which the latter knew nothing. True, as Member of Council, Gillespie had attended its debates and assented to its findings, but he had not read all the confidential papers that he, Blagrave, had. He saw Raffles every day and at all hours, whereas the Council only met once a week and Gillespie did not always attend. After his wound in June 1812, for instance, he was convalescing for months. So, said Blagrave, Raffles had a free hand and behind a façade of public service had been feathering his own nest. Besides being corrupt, he was quite unpractical. Many of his measures were ill-conceived and amateurish. The General, though unable to follow Blagrave in all the technicalities, for he was totally ignorant of economics and finance, became convinced that it was his duty on reaching Calcutta to expose the Lieutenant-Governor. The allegation which roused him the most was that Raffles had gone behind his back and written to Minto that he was unfit for the Java command. By the time Blagrave had finished his revelations, Gillespie was so angry that, with a rashness habitual to him, he even believed Blagrave had been wrongly dismissed and was an innocent man whose testimony could be entirely relied on. On reaching Calcutta in December 1813 he was given a rousing reception as a victorious general by his military friends, to whom he blackguarded Raffles and declared that the government ought to institute proceedings against him.

The situation at the time of his arrival was as follows. Lord Moira, Minto's successor, had landed at Calcutta on 4 October 1813, with his wife, the Countess Loudoun, and assumed office as Governor General the following day. Lord Minto had asked to be relieved in January 1814 but in the middle of 1813 had been informed by the Board that he was to hand over to Lord Moira in October of that year. Moira, a man of sixty, was a bosom friend of the Regent's. As an intimate in the Carlton House circle of that prince, he had become heavily in debt and asked the Regent to find him a lucrative appointment where he could save enough to pay his creditors. The Regent brought pressure to bear on the Board, Moira went out, Minto was recalled some three months before he planned to go. To atone for what was certainly an undeserved slight, Minto was made an Earl and his services to the Company were warmly acknowledged by a Resolution of the Court.

When he heard of his impending recall, Minto had felt nervous about his friend, Raffles's, prospects. The future of Java remained undetermined. Even Raffles's appointment as its Lieutenant-Governor had not yet been officially confirmed in London. He might suddenly find himself out in the cold, without a patron to look after him. To give him some security Minto ruled that in case he lost his present appointment, the Residentship of Bencoolen should be reserved for him. Bencoolen was a small place on the south coast of Sumatra, which had been a British trading settlement for a long time, but was now much less important than Penang. It was the best, however, Minto could think of; at least his friend would have an independent charge, better than having to revert to his substantive appointment in the Penang secretariat, a cruel declension after his brilliant conduct of Javan affairs. He got Moira to confirm this. In November 1813 he wrote to Raffles: 'I have had an early communication with Lord Moira concerning your appointment to Bencoolen; and I have the happiness to say that he acquiesced entirely in the arrangement that was made, and specifically in the propriety of your continuing to administer the government of Java until the future destiny of that Island should be fixed by the government at home. Believe me, ever most faithfully and affectionately yours.' Having done his best to protect the man he was so fond of, Minto embarked for home on 11 December, resolved to speak up for him also in London. It was on that very day that Gillespie came on the scene.

Gillespie would never have got a hearing had Minto still been in office. But now the coast was clear. All Lord Moira knew about Java was what he had heard in London, where Raffles was under criticism for having failed so far to balance his accounts. The Court and the Board were in no mood to help him out. When Moira left London in April 1813, the war was still at its crisis. The retreat from Moscow was over, but Napoleon, who had hastened back to Paris ahead of the remnant of his army, was raising another army. His defeat at Leipzig was five months away, his abdication and banishment to Elba a year in the future. Moira was instructed by the Board to exercise the strictest economy. He was to observe with special care the long-standing rule that extensions of territory were highly undesirable. More, he was directed to remit to London from the Company's reserves, very large sums in gold. No wonder one finds him noting in his Journal soon after his arrival that Java was the worst drain of all on the Company's resources. 'Raffles asks for 50,000 Spanish dollars monthly in addition to the prodigious sums we already contribute to his establishment.' He knew very well that Raffles was a remarkable man, who had been working in the closest collaboration with Minto since July 1810, and that Minto had the highest opinion of his rectitude, but he was prejudiced against him, a prejudice not uncommonly entertained by a new incumbent for the favourites of his predecessor, though to oblige Minto he had endorsed his wishes about Raffles's appointments.

Gillespie did not delay to bring forward his charges. On 25 December, only a fortnight after Minto sailed for England, he appeared before the Governor General in Council and was given a hearing. Though the charges that he brought against Raffles were on the face of them hardly credible, yet it seemed as hard to believe that Gillespie, a man of family, a general in the British army and greatly admired as a dashing leader in the field, could bring false charges against a colleague and senior in the government. Military society in Calcutta backed him; Lord Moira, a soldier himself who had served under Sir Arthur Wellesley, did not think it conceivable that so distinguished a soldier would sink to concocting a false case. What he alleged (and he had Blagrave to back him) must have some truth in it. There would have to be an inquiry and the first step was to frame an indictment and call on Raffles for an explanation.

On 26 February 1814 an East Indiaman arrived at Batavia with despatches from Calcutta wherein the impeachment of Raffles was set out. Raffles looked through the papers and handed them to Travers, who in his *Diary* records that he was dumbfounded. How could Gillespie 'have the villainy and duplicity' after saying goodbye with such protestations of goodwill 'to frame and fabricate a list of falsehoods'. And he denounces the impeachment as 'an infamous and disgraceful undertaking'. It was disgraceful of the Governor General in Council to have listened to such baseless slanders. Gillespie had produced no proof of his accusations. He had no papers in support nor any witnesses except Blagrave, a disreputable person with a grievance. Nevertheless, on this slender foundation the Governor in Council had drawn up no less than seventeen specific charges and called on Raffles for an explanation.

Raffles might have replied that before answering the charges he had the right to know what evidence, other than Blagrave's, the complainant had brought in support of his allegations. But judging it necessary to rebut the charges without a moment's delay, he set to work at once on a comprehensive survey of his administration (so lengthy as to make a volume when printed) which demonstrated, by documents, statistics, records, sworn statements, the utter nonsense of the charges. Calm and unperturbed, he laboured on his reply for nearly a month. Government House at Buitenzorg was as usual full of his guests. But, records Travers, 'not a visitor could perceive the slightest alteration in his manner; he was the same cheerful animated person they had always found him; at dinner and in the evening he appeared perfectly disengaged, and only seemed anxious how best to promote and encourage the amusement, and contribute to the happiness and enjoyment, of all around him.'

Were a detailed examination of the charges given here, the reader of today would skip it, and rightly so, since finally they were all acknowledged to be unfounded. Suffice it to say that thirteen of them had to do with the sale of government land already referred to, when Raffles, in urgent need of ready money to meet the expenses of his administration, decided, with Minto's sanction, to hold auctions, at which he himself bought some plots. Raffles, said Gillespie, bought cheaply and immediately sold at a large profit. The money received from the other buyers at the auctions he used to redeem the depreciated paper currency in such a way as to make a handsome profit for himself. The remaining four charges were to the effect that his failure to make Java pay was solely due to his incompetence.

Raffles had finished his lengthy refutation by the end of March, when he showed a copy of it to General Nightingall, Gillespie's successor in the Java command, who wrote to say that he agreed with every word of it and was ready to give any support which might be required. Raffles then sent a copy to the Governor General in Council by the hand of one of his secretaries, Assey, who arrived in Calcutta on 15 June, having been delayed on the voyage. He found that Moira was on tour a great distance away and could do no more than hand the papers to the Council. Another copy Raffles entrusted to Travers with instructions to leave immediately for London and present it to the Court of Directors. Travers arrived in England on 17 September 1814. By that date Napoleon had abdicated and was at Elba and the British government had already decided on the restoration to Holland of her island empire in the East. The Court had lost interest in Java and looked forward to its shortly being off their hands. When Travers presented the memorandum, they were disinclined to wade through it. The subject had become academic. As to whether Raffles had taken advantage of his position and made a fortune, there was no hurry to look into that. Consideration of the matter could be postponed until they received the Governor General's report. Travers was unable to get them to take any action, though he pleaded that delay would damage Raffles's character.

Death of Minto

Had Minto been in London, Travers would have gone to him, but he had died suddenly on 21 June, three months before Travers's arrival in England. His ship had come in on 19 May and his intention was to drive as soon as he could to his house in Scotland, where his wife and youngest daughter, whom he had not seen for seven years, were waiting. The celebrations following Napoleon's abdication in April delayed him. He had to appear at some important public functions. When he was about to start north his old friend Lord Auckland had a stroke and died, and he felt that he must attend the funeral. This took place at Beckenham, a twelve mile drive into the country. Before the procession reached the churchyard the sun had set. The evening sky clouded over and a drizzle began. Minto already had a cold; standing by the graveside in the wet made it worse. His impatience to rejoin his wife, however, was such that he refused to lie up and left for Scotland on 19 June, though by this time seriously ill. Pneumonia set in and he died on 21 June at Stevenage, thirty miles up the Great North Road. His body was brought back to London and buried in Westminster Abbey. He was adored by his family. Of his death his eldest son wrote: 'Any attempt must be vain to describe the overwhelming weight of this blow.' In the family's love for him 'were combined the warmest familiar affection, with admiration, respect and veneration'. In India no Governor General had before aroused such warm feelings, both among the servants of the Company and the general population, for 'the inestimable blessings of security, of order and of justice were his prime objects, and in all humanity was his guide', as was declared in a farewell address to him by the citizens of Calcutta. The news of his death did not reach Raffles until January 1815, seven months later, a blow of as overwhelming a weight as it had been to the Minto family. Raffles's nature being what it was, he felt

Minto's death even more as a personal loss than as one which endangered his own prospects, and wrote: 'Lord Minto was snatched away from the embraces of his friends and family at the very moment when he was about to receive the only reward which in this world could recompense his past labours' – the contemplation in tranquillity of a life's work nobly done.

In the *Memoir* compiled by Raffles's second wife, Sophia, after his death, occurs the sentence: 'At this period it pleased God to deprive Mr Raffles of some of his nearest and dearest connections.' The last word is explained in a footnote: 'Death of Mrs Raffles.' This is the only reference to Raffles's first marriage which occurs in her lengthy, detailed and well documented biography. Why she eliminated her predecessor is left to surmise. Was it delicacy or was it that she could not face the fact that the man she had loved for nine years had also loved another woman for nine years as ardently as he loved her? One can but record the fact that Olivia died in Java on 26 November 1814 at the age of forty-three. The climate had been too much for her. She had become very run down. Earlier in the year she fainted at a ball. She died very suddenly and was buried alongside the grave of Leyden in Batavia. On a cenotaph which Raffles erected to commemorate her at Government House, Buitenzorg, he inscribed the first verse of a love poem which she had addressed to Leyden soon after he left Penang to return to Calcutta in January 1806. It is not possible to resolve this little mystery with absolute certainty. The poem is romantic and highly emotional. She begs him in moving terms not to forget her. Raffles now inscribes her words on the cenotaph as if they came from him and were a prayer addressed to her, imploring her not to forget him in death, where she had gone to rejoin Leyden. How exactly did those three persons define their relationship to one another, the husband, the wife and the lover whom they both loved? It was evidently a relationship which suited them. Has one to do here with a romantic friendship or a *ménage à trois*? It cannot have been the latter, because the three were together only on two occasions – at Penang in 1805-6 for two and a half months, when Leyden stayed with the Raffleses, and for one month at Malacca where they were stationed in 1811. Leyden arrived at Malacca on Minto's staff *en route* for Java on 18 May 1811 and left on 18 June with Minto and Raffles for Java. Olivia remained at Malacca till she rejoined her husband in the autumn of the same year; by that time Leyden was dead. So she and he were together a total of three and a half months. The first period sufficed for an intense emotional relationship between them to develop. It was deepened by subsequent correspondence and exchange of poems. Raffles was not only a consenting party to this relationship; he encouraged it. The conclusion would seem to be that, as all three were romantic idealists, the Olivia-Leyden romance was of that kind.

Some three weeks before Olivia died another death occurred which certainly caused Raffles no grief. Gillespie, on whose charges the Governor General in Council had as yet passed no orders, though a year had passed, was killed in action in October 1814. He had been sent to reduce Kalunja, a stronghold from which the Gurkhas had been raiding the Company's territory. Knowing his character, Moira had taken the precaution to advise him that Kalunja should not be stormed until the artillery had adequately breached the fortifications. Gillespie, who had the fatuous belief that he bore a charmed life, disobeyed the Governor General's instructions to bombard, and indulged his taste for a flamboyant storm by himself leading the troops, like Bonaparte at Lodi, but without Bonaparte's luck. At the foot of the rampart he was killed. The Company's troops withdrew without taking the place. In reporting the reverse to London, Lord Moira made it clear that though, as a soldier himself, he admired Gillespie's intrepidity, he had no opinion of his commonsense.

Even with Gillespie's death, no decision on his charges was made. Neither India nor London had given the case proper attention and it was allowed to remain pending, a strain on Raffles's nerves and harmful to his reputation. It was another two years before the final verdict of the Court was published.

Chapter Nine

RAFFLES AS ORIENTALIST

Raffles's situation in 1814–1816 – his researches into Javanese history and archaeology – The Princess Charlotte – News reaches him of his supersession – Moira's character – Raffles relieved by Fendall leaves for England – his collections

Raffles remained Lieutenant-Governor of Java for two years after sending off in March 1814 his refutation of Gillespie's charges. His situation was peculiar. As ruler of Java, an island as large as England, he was far more independent than any modern governor of a similar territory, who is in daily touch by telegraph with his home government. He knew well enough that his immediate superior, Lord Moira, was not well disposed towards him nor were the Court and Board in London. But they took no action against him. A commission was not sent out to make inquiry on the spot. He was not suspended as a prelude to such an inquiry. Nor was he ordered to stop remodelling the administration. He was left to go on with his policy, but was aware that he had neither the confidence nor the backing of the Indian and London authorities in his reforms. There was no enthusiasm there for what he held to be a policy of justice, fair play and the encouragement of the individual. He was working in a sort of vacuum. The fate of the island remained in doubt.

His own future was equally undecided. His endeavours might lead nowhere. He might be disgraced. He was almost certain not to be rewarded. It seemed impossible to imagine that, even if the authorities admitted he was honest and meant well, they would applaud him, as Lord Minto had.

Nevertheless, his interest was quite unabated. He pushed on as energetically as ever, and this despite increasing ill health. Not only was his industry astonishing but his mind teemed with fresh ideas. As his grasp of eastern affairs increased, their trend became apparent to him and he began to think like a statesman.

Was England, he asked himself, not going to make use in the East of the advantages which her victory over Napoleon gave her in the West? Though she might be obliged to restore the eastern islands to Holland, was she to give the Dutch leave also to reimpose their monopolies and exclude British trade as in the past? That would be quixotism run mad. And there was the further point: The Dutch had not in fact owned all the islands; they had trading posts in them and managed to cajole or force the Sultans into letting them have their exportable products. What England should do, now that she had the power, was to make trade agreements with the sultans of such islands as Borneo, the Celebes, the Moluccas, agreements which the rendition of Java to the Dutch should not upset. The Dutch would be given back their property but not the right to exclude England from trading in the islands and coming to understandings with the sultans. And Raffles began feeling his way towards a system of alliances which would assure Britain new markets. Such a policy towards native rulers was contrary to the Company's policy in general, as it led to involvement in quarrels between rulers and the expense of sending troops to support one side. But Raffles, as he saw the future, considered it necessary.

Discovery of Borobudur

Besides the heavy work involved in changing the old administration and making diplomatic approaches to the outlying sultans, Raffles pursued his studies into the archaeology, zoology, botany and literature of Java. He had a quantity of helpers. Even the sultans were asked to write the history of their states. These researches provided the material for his *History of Java*, for which he began preparing at this time. Assistants reported to him their finds. He sent home to the Oriental Museum in the East India House specimens of animals, birds, insects and plants. He had all ancient sites surveyed. The report that a great temple had been discovered hidden in thick jungle near Jokyakarta, of which the Dutch knew nothing, much excited him and as soon as he could, he made the long journey there. The temple was Borobudur, built a thousand years back, regarded today as the most splendid of all Buddhist shrines of antiquity. Raffles's account of it in his *History of Java* shows that he did not know it was Buddhist, though the name means The Great Buddha; at that date very little was known about Buddhism, and its art was not distinguished from Hindu art. The stone reliefs at Borobudur, of which there are hundreds, seemed to him to represent scenes from Hindu mythology, though in fact they record the life of the Buddha. But he was captivated by it as a work of art. Indeed, its mood was bound to appeal to him. The carved scenes are sweet and gentle, with an atmosphere of the golden age, when men and animals went happily together, a mood close to his own.

Raffles was in frequent correspondence with William Marsden, one of the leading British orientalists of the day, a savant of sixty-two then resident in London. As a member of various learned societies, like the Royal Asiatic, and moving in circles which eagerly discussed any new piece of information about Far Eastern history and art, he took every opportunity of mentioning his friend, Raffles's, name. Men like Sir Joseph Banks, the President of the Royal Society, whose reputation as a savant dated from forty-five years back when, in his early twenties, he accompanied the great navigator, James Cook, to Tahiti, got to hear of him. That London society was already interested in him and prepared to receive him if he came to London is evident, too, from the Princess Charlotte's having let him know she would be pleased to accept Javanese ponies for her phaeton. He sent her six and also some furniture made from rare hardwoods. As the Princess Charlotte was the Regent's daughter, and heir to the throne of England in succession to her father, friendly acquaintance with her opened large possibilities for his future. If he reflected on the influence which these contacts gave him, he will have seen it as something to balance his lack of reputation with the Court of Directors. He was on the way to becoming a celebrity, but not as an administrator or a far eastern statesman. G. M. Trevelyan, in his *British History in the Nineteenth Century* (1922), writes of him as 'one of the greatest and best servants our Empire ever possessed. He was perhaps the first European who successfully brought modern humanitarian and scientific methods' to improve the lot of the native races of Asia. It was not in this guise, however, that he had attracted the notice of both learned and fashionable London society. That sort of celebrity came much later. London society was but faintly interested in Asian problems. But members of it were ready to be amazed at what was novel to them in the Asian scene. Raffles's dawning celebrity was due to his being recognized as the most gifted purveyor at the moment of this new information. Nevertheless, the fact of his being a far more cultivated man than his contemporaries in the service of the Company was the cause of so much envy that it did him officially more harm than good. Only a very exceptional chief like Minto could fully appreciate his character and talents.

Time passed. He still awaited the assurance that his answer to Gillespie's charges was accepted. At last in September 1815, eighteen months after he had sent off his refutation, he received a private letter from William Ramsay, son of his old chief of East India House days, and himself on the London staff of the East India Company. The letter stated Ramsay had learned that the Court in April 1815 decided to supersede him and also to cancel his reversion to Bencoolen on Moira's advice.

On this, Raffles wrote at once direct to the Earl of Buckinghamshire, the President of the Board, repeating what he had learned from Ramsay and saying: 'It is scarcely possible to conceive of a greater degree of injustice than what I have thus received at the hands of the Earl of Moira.' Not, however, until 18 January 1816, four months later, did he hear officially that the supercession reported by Ramsay was a fact. He received a very cold unpleasant letter from Moira announcing his recall. By November 1815 news of the battle of Waterloo (June 1815) had reached Java and also a report of the Anglo-Dutch convention of 13 August under which Java was to be returned to the Dutch. His appointment as Lieutenant-Governor of Java was therefore anyhow about to end. But Moira's letter made no reference to such an inevitable termination. Raffles was to be relieved by a certain John Fendall, who would hold office until the Dutch took over in a few months' time.

Moira's letter began by declaring that Raffles must be acquitted of those charges impugning his honesty, though his explanation of why he purchased lands at the auctions was not satisfactory. These purchases, together with the many instances of his mismanagement of affairs, sufficed to warrant his removal. However, as his moral character was not implicated, he might take up the minor responsibility of the Residency of Bencoolen. This was a concession, as Moira had originally advised against the appointment.

From the Governor General's letter and the letter appended to it from the Court, it is clear that both authorities saw Raffles as a *persona non grata* with the Dutch, to be cleared out of the way before they returned to take over, for the policy of the British government was to avoid any sort of unpleasantness with that nation, held to be a vital factor in the balance of power on which the safety of England depended and for the restoration of which she had fought Napoleon for some twenty years. It was thought likely to be unpleasant for the Dutch to arrive and find Raffles in charge. Had he not again and again made it clear that he considered their administration to have been unjust, oppressive and corrupt, as well as foolishly unsound? Moreover, as the letter from the Court pointed out, the new land revenue system, so hastily introduced, had served 'to alienate the minds of numerous individuals whose long established authority had been subverted by it'. It would be an affront to the returning Dutch to ask them to take over the government from a man who had insulted and caused damage to their nationals.

This was wholly a misconception on the part of the Court and the Governor General. The Dutch residents of Java had supported Raffles in his reforms. Two of their most distinguished officials had worked harmoniously on his Council. No Dutchman had endorsed Gillespie's charges. Raffles was on the best of terms with the entire Dutch community, whose notabilities he frequently entertained at his table and whose wives had become much attached to Olivia. In point of fact, before the British invasion of Java Dutch thinkers had urged some of the very reforms carried through by Raffles, notably a certain Dirk van Hogendorp. Furthermore, after the Dutch took over in 1816 they gave careful attention to Raffles's measures and, far from declaring them void, used them as guides in a new administration which they gradually evolved. He came eventually to be looked back on with veneration by many of them, as a man whose policy was distinguished by an endeavour to place the welfare of the native inhabitants above company profits.

These plain facts of the case show how very badly informed were the Court and the Governor General. The Court, disappointed that Java was not immediately a paying proposition, took the view that Raffles was an amateur philanthropist and gave him no time to prove that his policy was financially sound. They were not interested in his internal policies and, there is evidence to suggest, did not even read his long despatches. As for Moira, he had never met him, but had listened to the many slanders on his character emanating from military circles, who saw the clash with Gillespie in the light of a set against the army by a civilian. But it would be a mistake to think of Moira as a typical member of the military caste. In the first place he represented both the civil and military powers, being Governor General and Commander-in-Chief. Besides that, he was an able man with wide experience of civil life. One has only to look at his portrait by an unknown artist in the National Portrait Gallery; a remarkable expressive face confronts you, powerful yet sad, and not unkind. The same grieving dreaming look is to be detected in the Hoppner portrait in University College, Oxford. In his letter to Raffles he does not do himself justice. Some years later when he met him he found how wrong he had been, as will be related in its place. The only explanation of his mistake is that he had not taken the trouble, or had not had time, to go into the case thoroughly. As Commander-in-Chief he

had been continuously in the field from the date of his
assuming office in October 1813 till the date of his letter,
October 1815. First it was a war against the Gurkhas and then
the danger of the Pindari raiders and the great host of the
Mahrattas, militant central Indian powers of the most blood-
thirsty kind, who were leagued to drive the Company out of
India. These took another two years to subdue. His victory
over them delivered the Indian populace from violence,
spoilation and misery. What with the heat, exhaustion,
maddening reverses, heady triumphs, he had small inclination
to pore over the mass of papers relating to Java and the
Raffles case. At the time he was a man of sixty-one, far too
old for campaigning in tropical countries. It is hard to picture
this bosom friend of the Regent and habitué of Carlton
House, now elderly but obliged to lead huge sepoy armies
year after year over the burning Indian plains, when the
gaming clubs of Pall Mall might have been his battlefield. He
had been the Regent's Chamberlain and was his executor,
referred to in the Regent's will as 'My friend, the Earl of
Moira, whom I have ever most affectionately loved', and
enjoined 'ever to guard and protect for my sake my adored
Maria Fitzherbert'. He figures in many of the anecdotes told
of the Regent, as when he and Beau Brummell were drinking
alone with the Regent in Carlton House, the latter asked
Brummell to ring the bell. 'Your Royal Highness is close to
it,' replied Brummell. This offended the Regent, perhaps
from the tone of over-familiarity in which it was spoken, and
he would have ordered Brummell to leave the house, had not
Moira known how to soothe him. In short, Moira had an
immense experience of people of every sort. He would never
have been mistaken over Raffles and dismissed him, if he had
given proper attention to the matter. And if he had known
that Raffles had recently established by presents and letters an

acquaintance with the Princess Charlotte, daughter of his dear friend, the Regent, to have written to him the way he did would have been out of the question. The great Warren Hastings once emphatically stated: 'Lord Moira's understanding is both solid and brilliant.'* It was not spite or stupidity which led him into error but inattention.

Even so, it is not easy to account for his recall of Raffles. It was common knowledge that what Raffles had done in Java had been sanctioned by Minto. Minto knew all about his policy and specifically agreed that his bidding in the land auctions was unobjectionable. For Moira to censure Raffles was for him to censure his eminent predecessor. He did not record any reasons for declaring Raffles's reforms to be 'consecutively injudicious' and having the nature of 'persevering imprudence'.

Another consideration which should have given Moira pause was that two senior members of his Council, Neil Edmonstone and Archibald Seton, recorded minutes in favour of Raffles when the matter came before the Council. Seton's minute contained the following sentence with reference to the financial debit, the point which all along had worried the Court: 'That Mr Raffles has not succeeded in his endeavours may I think be attributed to the exhausted state in which he found the island, to the annihilation of its export trade, to a want of specie and to the fatal necessity of engaging in early and extensive wars against the Sultans.'

Moira, no doubt, may have felt that Raffles had not done too badly. He had been left as Lieutenant-Governor of Java for four and a half years, an appointment which he was very lucky to get considering he was only thirty at the time. Moreover, he was being let have Bencoolen. As his appointment was coming to an end in any case, he could not have

* Lord Curzon's *British Government in India*, Vol. II, p. 188.

held it for more than another two or three months. All in all, he had got out of the Gillespie business pretty well. No one had suggested that his administration of Java merited praise. Such was Moira's opinion at this time.

But this was not Raffles's view. He wrote at once to Lord Moira complaining that his lordship's letter was so phrased that acquittal had been dealt out with a sparing and doubtful hand. It was not clear whether he had been fully acquitted of the main charge of profiting from the land he bought at auction. He informed Moira that he intended to appeal to the Court and asked for copies of Edmonstone's and Seton's minutes. This letter was dated 27 January 1816 and he followed it up with another stating that his state of health precluded his taking up the Bencoolen appointment at once. His doctors strongly advised him to seek a change of climate and he proposed to take leave and return to Europe. He had been out east for ten years.

This was a very sound decision on his part. Not only his health demanded it, but also his interest, for in London with the influential support he had both in learned circles and society, he would have a much better chance of impressing the Court in his favour than he could hope to have by correspondence from the East.

Raffles was confined to bed when Fendall, his successor, arrived on 11 March, but managed to get down to the roadstead to meet him. Fendall turned out an agreeable man. He shared none of his superiors' prejudice against Raffles. After taking charge as Lieutenant-Governor he issued a notification in *The Gazette* that Raffles was to receive till he sailed the same courtesies and dignities as before, such as bodyguard, number of carriage horses, salutes, etc. He did not embark until 25 March. He had a great send-off. All public bodies, Dutch and native, presented him with flattering addresses.

Raffles Leaves Java for England

The British inhabitants, headed by the military, subscribed for a service of plate to be bought in London for him, and in an address expressed their lasting regard and declared their admiration for his private character and for the ability, justice and impartiality which had marked his administration.

His collection of manuscripts, carvings, textiles, plants, stuffed animals, insects, fruits and folk art was so large that it weighed thirty tons and was packed in upwards of two hundred cases. He had, as mentioned, already sent to museums and learned societies and zoos specimens of all sorts. What he now took with him was the bulk of his collection, which he was assured by his London correspondents would be viewed there with the greatest interest. Embarking with him were his two aides-de-camp, one of them Travers, the diarist and his great friend. Travers's account of the final departure contains these phrases: 'Mr Raffles was accompanied to the bank by all the respectable inhabitants of Batavia who took leave of him with tears in their eyes. The chief Chinese and Native inhabitants would not take leave of him till they had seen him on board, when they evinced the deepest grief on taking leave. All his intimate friends came off on board with him and here I am not capable of describing the distressing scene which took place.'

Chapter Ten

RAFFLES AND NAPOLEON

*Raffles visits Napoleon at St Helena – Waterloo – Hudson
Lowe – Countess Loudoun – Napoleon asked to meet her by
Lowe – Raffles's interview with Napoleon – Napoleon's
views on Java and Dutch – Princess Charlotte and Napoleon – Raffles lands in England*

The course taken was through the Straits of Sunda
between Java and Sumatra, the usual route for ships
sailing directly from Chinese waters to the Cape and
vice versa. The Cape was passed on 13 May 1816. They did
not put into Cape Town but sailed on to St Helena, which
was reached on 18 May, about eight weeks after leaving
Batavia.

St Helena had for centuries been a watering place for ships
on the eastern run, and now was very much in the news,
for there, confined on its heights, was the man who had
given his name to the age, the Napoleonic age. Napoleon
had arrived in St Helena on 17 October 1815, seven months
before Raffles put in there. Waterloo was only eleven months
back; 18 June 1815 was fresh in all minds. It seemed only the
other day that the Imperial Guard advanced in the summer
dusk to deal Wellington the knock-out blow, mounted the
slope of the ridge with solemn tread and shouldered arms,
to the rattle of their drums beating the *pas de charge*, and,

shattered before the British squares, fell back in disorder, while the terrible cry reverberated over the field: 'Nous sommes trahis!' 'By God, I don't think it would have been done had I not been there,' Wellington said to Creevy next day, a monosyllabic utterance of lapidary power. Though he saw himself master of a great event, he was humbled by the thought of what a close shave it had been. The victory had resounded over the waste of waters to East Asia, where Raffles was destined to give it amplitude. He was not in the hub of European history, but his position in Asiatic history-to-be was central. He would accomplish there what, added to Waterloo, would complete the design for the world's next hundred years, the hundred years of British hegemony. With Wellington he could murmur that it would not have been done had he not been there. No wonder, then, that he ardently desired to see the Emperor who had to fall before he could rise, to behold him 'abject and lost, under amazement at his hideous change'. Such were the echoes as he looked at the heights. But it was not to be easy to speak with the fallen angel.

Sir Hudson Lowe had only arrived the month before to take over the governorship of the island from Colonel Wilks, an East India Company man. He was a second-rate soldier of displeasing personality. After meeting him for the first time Napoleon is reported to have said: 'He had the eye of a hyena in a trap.'* Wellington considered him a very bad choice for a job requiring so much tact. One day Earl Stanhope said to the Duke that he supposed he had scarcely known Sir Hudson personally. 'Yes I did,' said the Duke in his downright way. 'I knew him very well. He was a stupid man . . . He knew nothing at all of the world.'† It was a pity Colonel Wilks had not stayed on. He was intelligent and

---

* *Napoleon, the Last Phase,* Lord Rosebery.
† *Conversations with Wellington,* Earl Stanhope.

well-read and knew who was who. His replacement by
Hudson Lowe irritated Napoleon, who remarked: 'Pourquoi
n'ont ils pas laissé ce vieux gouverneur? Avec lui je me serais
arrangé, nous n'aurions pas eu de querelles ' One of Lowe's
first acts was to annoy the Emperor in a matter concerning
the Countess Loudoun, the wife of Lord Moira, who passed
through St Helena on her way home from Calcutta about a
fortnight ahead of Raffles. In his *Private Journal* Lord Moira
records under date 1 January 1816: 'In a few days my wife
and children, the only comfort by which I am attached to
this world, are to embark for England.' And on 17 January
he has: 'I had now to bid adieu to all most dear to me. I have
been stupefied by the soreness of the blow.' When Lady
Loudoun went ashore at St Helena, Lowe asked her to dine
and wrote the following letter to Count Bertrand, the Emperor's Grand Marshal. 'Should the arrangements of General
Bonaparte permit it, Sir Hudson and Lady Lowe would feel
gratified in the honour of his company to meet the Countess
Loudoun at dinner on Monday at 6.0. They request Count
Bertrand to have the goodness to make known this invitation
to him and forward to them his reply.'* When Bertrand
showed Napoleon the letter and asked what answer he should
send, the Emperor's only remark was: 'It is too silly. Send no
reply.' It was, in fact, idiotic to suppose that the colossus, who
had bestrode Europe for twenty years, of whom the great
Duke himself declared: 'I can hardly conceive anything
greater than Napoleon at the head of an army. . . . There was
nothing like him. . . . His presence on the field made the
difference of forty thousand men,'† would be ready to dine
with Sir Hudson Lowe as General Bonaparte and be brought
up and introduced to a countess as if to a person he might

* *Napoleon, the Last Phase*, Lord Rosebery.
† *Conversations with Wellington*, Earl Stanhope.

think it a privilege to meet. He maintained, as Lowe knew, the etiquette of the imperial court at his residence, Longwood, and could only be met with if he chose to receive you.

That was what Lowe told Raffles when he asked permission to call on Napoleon. Application would have to be made through Napoleon's staff. If he was granted an interview, however, he was to address the Emperor as General Bonaparte and was not to speak to him with his hat off.

There exist two accounts of what transpired, one written by Travers in his *Diary* and the other by Raffles himself in a letter dated a few days later, which Wurtzburg prints in full. The accounts hardly differ. On the morning of the day after his arrival, 19 May, Raffles and his secretaries and doctor rode the eight miles into the interior to Count Bertrand's house. The Count gave them permission to walk in the grounds of Longwood and told them their best chance of seeing Napoleon was when he took his afternoon stroll there. About noon they met Count Las Casas, Napoleon's Councillor, who said that the Emperor was not yet dressed and would not be in the garden for some time. It was there that he invariably received visitors. It was impossible to announce them till he entered the garden. About three o'clock Napoleon was seen walking there with his suite. Las Casas informed him of the the visitors' presence and on obtaining his permission went to Raffles and told him to come forward.

Confronted thus with the Emperor, Raffles was shocked to see how shabby and broken down he looked. 'Now, then, behold me,' he writes, 'in the presence of certainly the greatest man of the age. I will not attempt to describe to you the feelings with which I approached him; let it suffice that I say they were in every way favourable to him. His talents had always demanded my admiration. . . . In a word I felt compassion for his present situation.'

Raffles and Napoleon

The letter goes on: 'On my nearer approach he stopped, took off his hat and slightly bowed and placed his hat under his left arm.' This seems to have been one of Napoleon's little mannerisms. It enabled Raffles to take off his hat, which he was glad to do, and led him to expect a few polite exchanges. He was surprised, therefore, when the Emperor, in the kind of authoritative tone used in interrogating a subordinate, rapped out at him a string of personal questions, demanding his name, ship, where he came from, followed by queries about Java and, before Raffles could answer, cross-examining Travers in the same abrupt fashion. After a few minutes he made a movement terminating the interview, turned his back and continued his stroll with his suite.

Raffles was put out by this reception, which he found rude. 'He treated us in the same manner as in his worst humour he was wont to treat his own inferiors.' Nevertheless he felt the enormous force of the Emperor's personality, and it alarmed him. He was captive but not tamed. The first impression of a broken spirit was erroneous. Napoleon, though his clothes gave him a countrified appearance, was still the despot. Indeed, he inspired horror. Raffles the humanitarian, the man of heart, left his presence much shaken. 'Believe me,' he wrote, 'this man is a monster.'

The conception of Napoleon as an ogre was, of course, very current. Thackeray, aged five, on his way home from Calcutta where he was born, was taken ashore at St. Helena this same year by the Indian servant in charge of him. They caught sight of Napoleon walking in the garden. 'That's he,' said the servant, 'that's Bonaparte. He eats three sheep a day and all the children he can lay hands on.'*

Though Napoleon's conversation with Raffles was confined to the staccato interrogations described, he held views

* *The Four Georges,* W. M. Thackeray.

about Java and its restoration to the Dutch comparable to Raffles's. Speaking on a subsequent occasion to Admiral Malcolm, who commanded the naval station, he said he could not understand why the British had got so little out of their victory. 'Probably for a thousand years such another opportunity of aggrandizing England will not occur. Nothing could have been refused to you. It was ridiculous to leave Batavia to the Dutch and return Mauritius and Bourbon to the French. Your ministers should have stipulated for a commercial monopoly in the seas of India and China. You ought not to have allowed the French or any other nation to put their nose beyond the Cape. At present the English can dictate to the world.'*

Raffles, as we know, had hoped against hope that Java would be retained. He had his humanitarian reasons; his political reasons were no less cogent. By returning it, not only was England relinquishing the new island empire which Minto and he had presented to her, but was taking inadequate precautions to insure that the Dutch did not reimpose their monopoly system and again shut the British out of the Island trade. The contention that England's safety depended upon a friendly power on the Scheldt and that the Dutch must necessarily be that power, seems never to have been acceptable to him. England was strong enough to have demanded what she wanted and have got it without having to strike a bargain. As will be seen later on, he remained convinced that steps had to be taken to make sure that the power attained by the victories of Trafalgar and Waterloo was made effective in the Far East, and British naval and commercial supremacy solidly established there. He did make sure of it and that was his great achievement in the political sphere.

There is one other curious link between Raffles and

* *Napoleon, the Last Phase*, Rosebery, p. 177.

Napoleon; both of them looked to the Princess Charlotte, the Regent's daughter. Raffles's reason for cultivating her favour we know. Napoleon believed he could count on her to get him out of St. Helena when she became Queen. A year after Raffles's visit, Count Gourgaud, one of Napoleon's staff, left the island to see what could be done on his master's behalf in Europe. Among others he was to see the Princess Charlotte. The Duke of Wellington may have had this in mind when he remarked to Stanhope in 1836: 'The death of the Princess Charlotte was probably by no means a misfortune to the nation. I fear she would not have turned out well.'

After the disconcerting audience with the fallen emperor, Raffles and his suite mounted their horses and rode as fast as the hilly road permitted down to the roadstead. Their ship was already under weigh, but they managed to board her before darkness fell, as Admiral Malcolm placed his barge at their disposal. Falmouth was reached on 11 July 1816, fifty-two days later. There Raffles disembarked with his suite and drove to London in a leisurely way, reaching it on 16 July. Next morning he reported his arrival at the East India House, feeling confident that he would get justice from the Court as soon as the Directors were in possession of the facts of his case. He was in high spirits and already felt much better.

Chapter Eleven

RAFFLES ACCLAIMED BY LONDON

Raffles had a great fund of happiness in his nature; he enjoyed everything. But his health had suffered from the climate of Java, from overwork, from grief at the deaths of Leyden, Minto and Olivia, and from anxiety about the charges left hanging over his head. If he could regain his health in his native air, see his big book published and be recognized as a man of intellect, get a complete acquittal from the Court and fortify himself with new friends, he would be quite his animated self again. He loved meeting people. In Java he was always the gayest at the parties he gave, even if not feeling too well. His popularity was due not only to his charming manners, easy way with people of all classes, but to the genuine warmth of his heart. London was about to lionize him, though he did not know it, and he was bound to to enjoy the experience immensely.

His first step was to secure a good address, which he found at 23 Berners Street, a large house. There he unpacked the two hundred cases which were landed at the London docks a few days after his arrival. He engaged a staff of servants, for he had only brought one Malay servant with him, and acquired a carriage and pair with liveries for the grooms and smart harness for the horses. Indeed, it was such a handsome equipage, wrote his first cousin, Dr Thomas Raffles, that when he went to call on his aunt, who had a modest dwelling near Spitalfields market in Princelet Street, he told his coachman to wait some distance off and, so as not to flaunt his affluence and position, walked to No. 14, her door, which he pushed open without ceremony, as he used to do when a clerk in the East India House, and entering her parlour-kitchen sat down in the old arm-chair he remembered so well, and in his affectionate way reminded her of how ambitious he was as a youth when he used to tell her he would be a Duke before he died. He had already been to see his mother, to whom all these years he had made an annual allowance of £400, a figure representing perhaps five times what it does today. Minto had calculated that he ought to be able to save £4,000 every year from his salary as Lieutenant-Governor of Java, and though he had not saved that amount, which in five years would have amounted to £20,000 (£100,000 today), he was certainly at this moment well supplied with money. His relations found him very pale and thin, but were immensely delighted to see him back.

Marsden, his old friend and correspondent, and Sir Joseph Banks, the President of the Royal Society, with others such as Sir Everard Home, the King's physician and a Fellow of the Royal Society, had been apprised of his arrival and when he called on them and invited them to inspect what his cases contained, the news went round London and invitations came in. But before settling to a round of visits he took the advice of his doctors and went to Cheltenham, as at that date drinking the waters there was held to be the best cure for the liver complaints from which all persons returning from the tropics were assumed to suffer. He spent all August 1816 at the cure. The waters did him no particular good but he met Sophia, daughter of a Mr Watson Hull of the County Down, who had come over from Ireland for the waters, and fell in love with her. In his *Diary* Travers describes her as 'affectionate and sensible, though not very handsome'. She was thirty years of age; Raffles was still very young, only thirty-six.

By 12 September he was back in London, and set to work to write his *History of Java*. As he had copious notes and drafts of some parts, he went ahead very fast and managed to get it printed as he went along, chapter by chapter. The Fellows of the Royal Society, aware of the book's forthcoming publication, began to introduce the author to their circle. It is from this date, October 1816, that he made his first entry into fashionable society. We hear of him, for instance, being invited to witness the opening of parliament by the Prince Regent on 28 January 1817, an occasion among others when the Regent's carriage was stoned by the mob. Now fifty-five years of age, the Prince had long been London's chief topic of conversation. Since the age of eighteen he had progressed from one scandal to another, each more thrilling for the gossips than the last and each the source of strings of anecdotes. He left Perdita Robinson, immortalized by Gainsborough,* and married and left Maria Fitzherbert, took up

* In the Wallace Collection, considered one of Gainsborough's principal masterpieces.

with the Countess of Jersey, and in 1795 at his father, George III's instance, agreed to marry the Princess Caroline of Brunswick. Their first meeting on the day she came over from Germany provided Sir James Harris (later Lord Malmesbury) with one of the good stories in the *Malmesbury Diaries*. After embracing her, the Prince retreated and called out: 'Harris, I am not well. Pray get me a glass of brandy.' It appears that the Princess did not wash as carefully as he required, for he was very particular on that score and expected a careful *toilette de propriété*. He had to marry her, however, because George III refused otherwise to pay his huge debts, but spent his wedding night lying drunk in the grate. The tale of how he received the news of Waterloo was one which it amused the Duke of Wellington to relate: 'The Prince Regent was that day dining at Mr Appen's, a merchant,' the Duke told Stanhope. At ten p.m. the Duke's Waterloo despatch reached London. The Cabinet was at Lord Harrowby's in Grosvenor Square and the postchaise and four, with eagles sticking out of the windows, drove there. Thence, near midnight, the chaise went on to Mr Appen's, where they found the Prince Regent still at table. 'He must have been drinking hard that day,' the Duke went on and, bursting into a laugh, quoted from the French play *Bergami*: 'Diable, comme il boit! Absolument, comme un ancien postillon retiré.'

Though the Prince Regent would not do for royalty today, to think of him as merely a debauchee is erroneous. He was a highly intelligent man, a personality, well educated, a linguist, a patron of the arts, who stamped on the period a style, the Regency style, was alive to what was happening in the world of letters, a friend of Charles James Fox, Burke and Sheridan, and an admirer of Jane Austen's novels. The décor of Carlton House and the Brighton Pavilion were his creations. Indeed, he was more broadly cultivated than any person who has occupied the throne of England since his time. He showed his perspicacity and independence when, as will shortly be related, he came forward and in the most public manner commended Raffles's achievements, and rewarded him, a line his employers, the Court of Directors, had never thought of taking. Raffles, of course, was known to him as one of his daughter, the Princess Charlotte's, friends. There can be little doubt that she had urged her father to take notice of him.

As an indication of the way things were to go we find that on 3 February he was invited to attend the Regent's levee at Carlton House. One of those present was the statesman, George Canning, a future Prime Minister, who had recently succeeded the Earl of Buckinghamshire as president of the Board of Control, the department of government which oversaw the policy of the Court of Directors. Raffles was presented to him, an introduction which, coming as it did in the elegant surroundings of Carlton House, did him far more good than would have an interview in Canning's office. It seems that Canning asked him to let him have his views in writing on the policy to be adopted in eastern waters consequent on the return of their possessions to the Dutch, and in due course Raffles sent him a paper entitled *Our Interests in the Eastern Archipelago*.

Two months before Raffles arrived in England the Princess Charlotte, then nineteen, had married Prince Leopold of Saxe-Coburg. They were given Claremont Park in Surrey as their residence, the house bought by Clive in 1768 when he returned from India. Raffles was a constant visitor there during the spring of 1817, for the Princess and her husband became much attached to him. At this time he gave her more Javanese tables and chairs, which she put in her dining

and drawing-rooms. When her grandmother Queen Charlotte, wife of old mad George III, heard of this, she said she
would like to call on Raffles to see his collection of eastern
objets d'art. It was arranged, however, for them to meet at the
Countess of Harcourt's house, a lady-in-waiting and friend
of Raffles's. There the Queen said to him: 'I heard wonderful
things of the treasures you have brought back from Java,'
adding that everyone particularly admired the beautiful
tables which he had given her grand-daughter. Dr Thomas
Raffles, who records the incident in his *Memoirs*, makes
Raffles reply how greatly honoured he would be at Her
Majesty's acceptance of a bit of such furniture. On her readily
assenting, he ordered a pair of tables which were being
made for Sir Joseph Banks to be sent forthwith to her
instead.

When the Court of Directors heard, as they did at once,
that their Mr Raffles, whom they had treated with such a lack
of consideration, was consorting with the Queen, with the
Princess Charlotte, the future Queen as was anticipated, with
George Canning, head of the Board that controlled them,
not to speak of other friends among the aristocracy and
ruling class, they decided it was time to send him a civil letter
and did so at the end of February 1817. It began by reiterating,
though in a more final manner than heretofore, the Court's
belief 'in the utter groundlessness of the charges exhibited
against him in so far as they affected his honour'. They were
in entire agreement with Mr Edmonstone's minute that all
his measures 'sprang from motives perfectly correct and
laudable'. This included the land auctions, though perhaps it
had been indiscreet of him to buy land himself. Let that pass,
however. As to the wisdom of some of his reforms, the
Court asked to be excused from expressing an opinion. It
seems to have still believed that to support his reforms might

offend the Dutch and appear as meddling in affairs which were no longer the Court's business. The letter ended by confirming his lien on the Bencoolen appointment, which would in his case be ranked and paid for as a Lieutenant-Governorship, though hitherto only a Residency.

So at long last ended a case which had been kept pending three and a half years since Gillespie made his charges in 1813. But satisfactory though the letter was as a whole, it did not contain one word of praise. Moreover, Bencoolen, as the Court well knew, was the back of beyond, quite outside the main movement of island affairs. The Directors may have reflected that once there Raffles could give no further trouble. It was an out-station of the remotest sort. Nothing happened or could happen there. Raffles would be got rid of. But a man of genius is not, as they discovered, so easily got rid of. Moreover, he was already formulating wide plans in the paper he was writing for George Canning, plans which could be set in motion from Bencoolen.

On 22 February he married Sophia Hull. The engagement had been a secret, the wedding was quiet. Writing to inform his cousin Dr Raffles of the event, he said that she had 'neither rank, fortune nor beauty' but possessed every qualification of the heart and mind to render him happy. Meeting as he did women of rank, fortune and beauty in the high society he was now frequenting and where he was already such a favourite, he might, had he been of a calculating nature, have paid court to one of them and looked for an appointment through her family's influence more attractive than the Lieutenant-Governorship of Bencoolen. There is some evidence to suggest that the Princess Charlotte had hinted she would get him shortly a baronetcy and that he could look forward confidently to a peerage, with the Indian Governor Generalship to follow, when she became Queen of England. Some ambitious men would have seen it as the wrong moment to marry a woman unconnected with the English ruling class. Sophia's family belonged to the Irish landed gentry. The Irish landed gentry had, no doubt, the manners of an upper class of first distinction. The Duke of Wellington's family, the Wellesleys, were of that class. But they had no influence whatever in London high society. Raffles's idea, however, did not run that way. He married Sophia Hull because he loved her. It was a love match, not a marriage of convenience. He was right in thinking he would never regret it. He was to be very happy with her despite all sorts of difficulties and disasters. After a short honeymoon at Henley he was back in Berners Street on 3 March.

London continued to lionize him. On 20 March he was elected a Fellow of the Royal Society. At his first reception there he made the acquaintance of the Duke of Somerset, who took a strong liking to him at once and invited him to his house. The Duchess became, after the Princess Charlotte, his closest friend in London. His correspondence with her is a valuable source for his biography.

Three weeks after his election as F.R.S. his *History of Java* was published in two volumes. It was dedicated by permission to the Prince Regent. In the dedication he declares that literature and the arts and sciences have been most conspicuously promoted during the Prince's regency, noted also for its justice and humanity. The Prince Regent will therefore be interested in the author's depiction of Javanese culture and glad to know that for nearly five years as Lieutenant-Governor he did everything in his power to make happy a mild and simple people, sure that in doing so he was carrying out his Prince's wishes. This assumption that Raffles had the approbation of the Prince Regent in the policy of reform, for which he had been rebuked by the Court and even now was not commended, must have been supported by assurances either directly from the Regent or through the Princess Charlotte. The implication was that the Regent favoured what the Court of Directors had not; that, in short, the monarchy was behind Raffles in what he had done. The Court of Directors would have to bear this in mind for the future. So would Lord Moira under whom he would still be at Bencoolen. In Lord Moira's case the approbation of the Regent would have even greater weight, since the Regent was his most intimate friend. Altogether, it was a cleverly drafted dedication.

The *History of Java*, modelled on Marsden's *History of Sumatra*, published seven years before, contains everything that Raffles and his assistants had been able since 1811 to discover about Java, its ancient history, its peoples, languages, arts, zoology, botany, as well as an exposure of the Dutch mercantile system, revealed as disgracefully oppressive and financially ruinous, compared with the new, free, humane and economically sound administration which the British had introduced. The book's encyclopaedic scope made it a vast contribution to western knowledge of the East Indies. It provided precisely what the Royal Society sought to foster and showed Raffles to be an orientalist of the first rank. Coming out the moment it did when London was making much of him, it immediately increased his celebrity. He had invitations to dine out every night. Unfortunately he kept no diary and, though usually a good correspondent, wrote few letters so that the names of most of those whom he met are not on record.

A month later he received a command to attend a levee at Carlton House on 29 May. The Prince Regent had made up his mind to give him the recognition which he so well deserved. We rely for what happened on a letter written by Dr Thomas Raffles, his cousin, who appears to have been present at the levee. After various persons had been presented to the Regent in accordance with the usual levee routine, it came to Raffles's turn to be brought up. At this point the Regent made it clear that something more than a polite exchange was to take place. He motioned to his suite to gather about him and intimated that he intended to address the company in general. Though no longer the handsome dandy of twenty years earlier, for he had become stout and bloated, his manners were delightful. The speech he made lasted twenty minutes. He began by saying that he had read the greater part of Mr Raffles's two volumes 'and in the most handsome manner expressed his approbation of the work, thanking him for the entertainment and information he had derived from the perusal'. He went on to speak of Raffles's administration, with the principles of which he was in full accord. In his view Raffles had rendered eminent services to his country. Concluding his remarks, he caused him to kneel and conferred on him a knighthood.

Soon after this Raffles toured the continent in his own carriage, his companions consisting of Sophia, his sister Mary Anne, his cousin Dr Raffles, and Sophia's brother, a family party, for Raffles was always a great family man as well as one with a host of friends. The party visited Paris, the scene of such splendours and miseries since the Revolution in 1789. For a person of his intellectual curiosity and vivid sensibility it was a wonderful experience to walk those streets and remark the triumphal monuments of a great emperor, whom a few months earlier he had spoken with, a captive on a lonely island. Traces of Napoleon Bonaparte were everywhere, on the pillars, for instance, of the church of St. Roch in the Faubourg St. Honoré, where one could detect the marks of his grapeshot fired on the famous 13 Vendemiére (5 October 1795), when aged twenty-six, he mowed down the mob, the first step in his giddy climb to power. The year

1795 was the very one that Raffles had entered the East India House, a friendless boy of fourteen. The Corsican had fallen, he was rising. On the ruin of the Corsican's plans to found an oriental empire, he was aspiring to open to Britain new realms in the East.

The party returned via the Netherlands, for Raffles was anxious to make the acquaintance of Falck, the Dutch colonial minister, and get some news of what was happening in Java. He had heard that Cranssens, the Dutchman who had served on his Council and for whom he had a great liking, was being slighted by the new government for having been too anglophil at the time of the hand-over by the British to the Dutch. At a dinner to which Falck invited him, Raffles assured the minister that no more loyal Dutchman than Cranssens ever existed and begged that he be treated fairly. This plea was typical of Raffles, who was very faithful to his friends, whoever they were. He was also invited to dinner by the King, whose son, the young Prince of Orange, had served on Wellington's staff and whom the Regent first selected as a suitable husband for the Princess Charlotte, then seventeen, but with whom she would have nothing to do, as he was so ugly, stupid and untidy. Raffles left the Netherlands with the feeling that the Dutch in Java were not going to be as easy-going neighbours for him in Bencoolen as he might reasonably have expected. Falck and the King had been pleasant enough, but it was clear that the Dutch, who were wretchedly poor after their misfortunes, intended to get all they could out of the Islands, and considered this could better be done by reimposing their monopolies and keeping out the British than by an open trade.

The middle of October was fixed by Raffles for his departure east. During August he took Sophia over to Ireland to say goodbye to her people in the County Down and on the way back stayed a few days with the Duke and Duchess of Somerset at Maiden Bradley, their country seat. By 12 September they were in Berners Street again. On 23 September Raffles – now Sir Stamford Raffles, for that was the style he had chosen, preferring his second name, Stamford, to his first, Thomas, so as to avoid confusion with his cousin Dr Thomas Raffles – was invited to take the chair at a dinner in the City. One of the guests was Henry Ellis who had returned to England only the month before from China, where he had gone as Third Commissioner of the embassy headed by Lord Amherst, the object of which was to obtain for England from the Emperor Chia Ch'ing trade concessions at Canton and the right to be diplomatically represented at Peking. The embassy had failed, because the Chinese government, convinced that the traditional policy of keeping the West at arm's length was the most prudent course, as closer contact would have a disruptive effect, was unwilling to modify the rules regulating trade and acted in such a way that Amherst had to return without seeing the Emperor. As negotiations had led nowhere – Lord Macartney's embassy of 1793 had been equally unsuccessful – it was becoming clear that only force or a show of force would make the Chinese give way; in short, the China trade, a trade of the utmost importance to England, could not prosper and expand until Britain was able to bring her lately won naval supremacy to bear in Chinese waters. That the paper which Raffles was submitting to George Canning entitled 'Our Interests in the Eastern Archipelago' took this fundamental factor into account shows with what speed and acumen he had seized upon the essential. Now on 23 September, a month before he set out for Bencoolen, and a new cycle of adventures, he meets Henry Ellis at dinner and has opportunity for an exchange of views with the man who knew more about the requirements of the

China trade than anyone else. Ellis's handsome volume *Journal of the Proceedings of the Late Embassy to China* was published before the end of the year. Besides the main conclusion to be drawn that England could not succeed by negotiations unbacked by force, it contained other matters of close interest for Raffles, for the embassy had touched at Java both going and returning. It had arrived at Batavia in June 1816, when Mr Fendall was in process of handing over to the Dutch, and passed through again in April 1817 when the Dutch flag had been hoisted, though Fendell was still on the island. Ellis had formed a high opinion of Raffles's Javan administration from what he heard there. At the city dinner of the twenty-third 'Mr Ellis arose', wrote Travers in his *Diary*, 'and in a most elegant and appropriate speech paid Sir Stamford's administration a very high compliment'. He paid him further compliments in his book, a publication as important as the *History of Java*, the two together being probably the books which aroused the greatest interest in 1817. In his book Ellis has: 'The separation between the natives of Java and the British will be matter of mutual regret. The enlightened policy . . . introduced by Mr Raffles had begun to find its reward . . . and at once liberated the commerce and agriculture of the island from the fetters of mercantile oppression. The colonial government, under his administration, appeared as the sovereign claiming a fair proportion of the resources of the country and not as the owner of a plantation, coercing his slaves to labour beyond their physical strength, for the gratification of his insatiable avarice. . . . It is to be hoped that the system of government introduced by the British will not be abandoned nor the inhabitants, now accustomed to better days, be thrown back to the miseries of political and commercial oppression.'

Coming as this did from a man of some position, who

could be termed an impartial observer fresh from the scene, Ellis's opinion amounted to a tribute which could not but be useful to Raffles as confirming the opinions of his friends and giving pause to those who sought to belittle him.

A week or so after the City dinner Queen Caroline asked him to spend an evening with her at Frogmore. There he met Lord Amherst himself. Besides the topic of the embassy, Amherst had a story to tell which Raffles will have found thrilling, the story of how on the voyage back from China his ship was wrecked some 300 miles from Java, how the passengers and crew had to take to the boats, and how some of them were in great danger from pirates. As he listened, Raffles could not have imagined that he would himself have a similar experience in a few years.

About this time he had his portrait painted by G. F. Joseph, A.R.A., the portrait now in the National Portrait Gallery, where it hangs beside those of Clive and Warren Hastings, with Lord Moira and Sir Joseph Banks nearby, and the Princess Charlotte on a wall adjoining. The artist shows him dressed in knee-breeches, a high-shouldered black coat and an elegant stock, clothes he might have worn as Lieutenant-Governor of Java, though more probably English levee dress, as the landscape behind has an English air. Beside him on the table are antique Javanese carvings. He seems in perfect health. He is good-looking, his eyes thoughtful, the mouth and chin determined, the expression at once dignified and charming. In July 1817 he was thirty-six.

About now he met William Wilberforce for the first time, and became his life-long friend. Wilberforce, who was twenty-two years his senior, had begun his struggle to abolish slavery by a motion in the House of Commons as far back as 1789, when Raffles was a child, but it was not until 1811, the year Raffles went with Minto to Java, that Wilberforce managed to get passed a Bill making it a felony punishable with transportation to carry slaves from Africa to the West Indies or elsewhere, an Act which ended the slave trade as far as the British were concerned. Wilberforce was now striving to take the matter the rest of the way and get a bill passed emancipating all existing slaves in British dependencies. He did not live to see this happen, as he died in 1833, a year before the Emancipation Act of 31 July 1834. Raffles had a natural revulsion from slavery. He had never been in doubt of its being an abomination to drag a human being from his home, sell him overseas where he was forced to work for nothing, was unprotected by the law and could be beaten to death without trial. Trade in slaves had at last after years of controversy been declared criminal, but the thousands of slaves already on British plantations continued as before. Raffles was ardently in favour of their emancipation. Such sentiments, though growing more widespread, were by no means common. The East India Company, for instance, did not entertain them. Raffles's efforts on behalf of slaves in Sumatra were to get him into trouble with the authorities.

With the date of his departure for Sumatra now close, it was time for him to bid the Princess Charlotte farewell and he went down to Claremont for that purpose. The Princess was expecting her first child who, had he survived, would have been King of England and there would have been no Victorian era. Dr Raffles records in his *Memoirs* the following scene. At a certain moment the Princess's husband, Prince Leopold of Saxe-Coburg, said: 'Sir Stamford, the Princess and myself are much indebted to you for the many expressions you have given us of your regard. Allow me to put this ring upon your finger as a token of our united regard.' The Princess was looking over his shoulder when he said this and in the lively manner for which she was known put in: 'And I request that you will sometimes wear it for my sake.' It was a ring with a big diamond, which Dr Raffles estimated was worth £400.

In all these circumstances – close friendship with royalty, esteem by the leading savants of the day, cordial acquaintance with George Canning, head of the Board, exoneration by the Court, an effectionate acquaintance with members of the ruling class – one asks why Raffles was leaving the centre of affairs and going out east again, this time to an appointment of far less importance than in Java. His close friends had urged him to remain in England; his health would not stand another stay in the tropics. Apart from the Princess's plans for his future, the Regent or Somerset or Banks would not leave him in the lurch. He had enough money for the moment. The answer is that he was going East again because he himself wished to go. He believed that he had a mission there. English power and influence must be established in the Archipelago and the China sea. He was convinced it was the Dutch intention to frustrate this. The policy of the Court and the Board was not vigorous enough. Unless he went out and saw to it, the opportunity would pass. The Dutch could be circumvented, but only if counter action were taken in time He was beginning to see how this could be done. If necessary he would present the Court with a *fait accompli*. A tide was setting in that would carry him to fame, if he took it at the flood.

The Memorandum on how to secure British interests in the Archipelago, which he had submitted at Canning's request, disclosed what measures he thought were necessary. Penang and Bencoolen were too distant from the centre of Dutch activities to be effective. There should be a third station, so situated that it would halt Dutch plans for interrupting and circumscribing British commerce. That third station should be at the eastern exit of the Straits of Malacca. Thereabouts were groups of islands lying off the point of the Malay peninsula. The settlement should be on one of those islands and command the passage from the Indian to the Chinese seas. The Memorandum named in particular an island or group called Rhio, situated a few miles south of the place where some centuries before a large walled city called Singapore had stood, separated from the Malay mainland by a narrow strait. The right course, the memorandum concluded, was to occupy Rhio or some other island in the mouth of the Straits before the Dutch did so.

Though the Court and the Board were insistent that nothing should be done to annoy the Dutch and endanger the post-Napoleonic settlement of Europe, for which England had striven so long and whose stability was of major importance, it was decided before Raffles left to give him certain general advisory duties in addition to his administrative work at Bencoolen. Writing later to the Chief Secretary of the Governor General, Raffles recalled what these duties were: 'I left England under the full impression that I was not only Lieutenant-Governor of Bencoolen but in fact Political Agent for the Malay States,' the position of adviser which he had held in 1810 under Minto. He was to report on all happenings throughout the vast Eastern Archipelago and was given to understand that 'it was the wish of the authorities in England that I should check the Dutch influence from extending beyond its true bounds.' How exactly he was to do this was not defined nor was he given a free hand to act, if an occasion arose which he deemed required him to act. His instructions were thus somewhat imprecise but appeared to him sufficient warrant for what he intended to try to do, which was to outwit the Dutch. In one of his letters he refers to Bencoolen as his Elba; like Napoleon he intended to escape from its confines. The half sanction he had been given was enough. He would risk taking responsibility for the rest.

On 23 October 1817 he embarked for Bencoolen on the *Lady Raffles*, a new ship which the Company had placed at his disposal, accompanied among others by his wife Sophia, his faithful secretary Travers, who also had recently married an Irishwoman who was with him, by Mrs Grimes a nurse, Sophia's brother William, a surveyor, and Arnold a botanist recommended by Sir Joseph Banks. A large collection of domestic animals, birds and plants was on board.

With adverse winds and storms they did not get clear of the Channel till 21 November, a month being wasted in putting in and out of Falmouth. At that port the news reached them that the Princess Charlotte had died on 5 November after giving birth to a stillborn child. Raffles wrote to the Duchess of Somerset on 9 November: 'An unexpected event has occurred, it has shocked me beyond measure – I dare not dwell on it.' Charlotte's death was a disaster for him comparable to Minto's. Dr Raffles confirms in his *Memoirs*, published in 1864, what has already been hinted at: 'The loss of the amiable Princess . . . touched him most tenderly, for he had a sincere regard for her, beyond any consideration of rank, or wealth, or honour, to which he might have attained, had both their lives been prolonged. No doubt was entertained at the time that if she had survived he would have been Governor General of India; while she would have been but too much delighted to have raised him to the peerage in that capacity.'

Chapter Twelve

RAFFLES'S LIEUTENANT-GOVERNORSHIP OF BENCOOLEN

Voyage to Bencoolen – Birth of Raffles's daughter Charlotte – Description of Bencoolen and Sumatra – Raffles's reforms – his tours in the interior of the island – his discovery of a giant flower – Sophia is taken for a spirit – Anecdote of a tiger – The jungle Chiefs ask for British protection – Dutch fear Raffles's influence with Chiefs

It took the *Lady Raffles* four months to get to Bencoolen, which was reached on 22 March 1818. No stop was made *en route*. Writing afterwards in her *Memoir* of what Raffles did during the long days at sea, Sophia has: 'Sir Stamford never relaxed his occupations – he regularly devoted his mornings to study, read and wrote on serious subjects till evening, when he read aloud some books of poetry.' We do not know the poets that he found to his taste, but imagine the romantics will best have suited his character. If so, he had a a rich choice among his contemporaries, for Wordsworth and Coleridge, Keats and Shelley, Byron and Scott, Landor and Southey, Moore and Crabbe, were all alive at this time.

Though Raffles was never bored, the tediousness of four months on a small ship that called at no port must have been great. However, one event, which in the confined quarters will have been exceptionally trying, was at least an escape from monotony. Sophia gave birth to a girl when they were southward of the Cape, fortunately in a moderate sea. Raffles had his doctor with him and with Mrs Grimes's assistance Sophia was delivered without mishap. He christened the baby Charlotte, after the Princess. One of his companions, a young Malay nobleman who had accompanied him from Java, made a suggestion. There was a Malay name, Tunjong Segara (the Lily of the Sea), which would be most appropriate, he said. So little Charlotte was given this name too. In a letter Raffles wrote during the voyage to the Duchess of Somerset he says that all is well with his Noah's ark, 'the cows, dogs, cats, birds, the latter singing around me, and my nursery plants thriving beyond all expectation'. But like all travellers when evening falls his heart melts at the thought of dear friends far away. 'What a waste of waters now lies between us, and yet the distance daily widens, and will widen still until half the world divides us.'

Though his reading of Marsden's *History of Sumatra* and hearing Marsden talk of Bencoolen had given him some idea of the place, the first sight of it was a shock. Immediately before his arrival an earthquake had severely damaged the house he was to occupy and a lot of other buildings. The Resident, who should have been there to meet him, had gone off some months before on sick leave and left affairs in the hands of a subordinate, who was incompetent. The damaged houses were not his fault, but the roads, impassable with mud or overgrown with rank grass, were due to his neglect. When Raffles reached Government House he found, as it had been unoccupied since the Resident left and no caretaker had been put in charge, that ravenous dogs and stinking polecats had taken up their quarters in it. He, his family, secretaries and suite, had to accommodate themselves as best they could until the damaged houses could be repaired and

cleaned. It was a dismal situation after a long and uncomfortable voyage, especially for the women, Sophia and Mrs
Travers and Mrs Grimes. Writing to Marsden Raffles
declared: 'This is without exception the most wretched place
I ever beheld. I cannot convey to you an adequate idea of the
ruin and delapidation which surrounds me.' But at no time
in his chequered career was Raffles depressed for long. He set
to work at once with energy and enthusiasm and soon he and
his party were in tolerable comfort.

It might be supposed that in so miserable an out-station
there would be nothing to do except attend to routine
business. Had he taken it easy the authorities in London
would have been quite content. But Raffles had not come out
to Bencoolen, a four months' voyage, 14,000 miles, to do
nothing. He had a multitude of plans in his head.

Sumatra is a thousand miles long, its area double that of
Java, and was part of the vast Eastern Archipelago over
which the Dutch claimed a general suzerainty. They had
never occupied, in an administrative sense, any part of it
and were concerned only to obtain from the ruling sultans,
as in Java, products of the soil in demand in Europe, particularly coffee. They had collecting posts along the coast. The
central parts of the island were inhabited by tribes, some of
them savages, some even cannibals. The north-west end was
the independent Moslem sultanate of Achin, a powerful and
more advanced state. Bencoolen had been maintained by the
British as a trading post since 1685, when the Dutch did not
dispute their entry. It lay one hundred and eighty miles
north-west of the Straits of Sunda, in the middle of a narrow
strip of coastline, three hundred miles long, recognized from
the first as a British preserve. The town itself was protected
by a fort called after the Duke of Marlborough. This British
trading post was run on the same lines as the Dutch posts.

Sufficient coffee, at a price low enough to insure a good profit when exported, was bought by agreement with the local chiefs, who obliged their subjects to grow it. It had been a commercial failure. The coffee export left an annual deficit of £100,000 to be met by drafts on the government in Calcutta. Bencoolen's only value was as an occasional port of call for British ships sailing via the Cape to China through the Straits of Suna; it was useless for the Calcutta-Canton run which was by the Straits of Malacca. The foreign population consisted of the military (a small force of sepoys under British officers), convicts transported from India, some two hundred company slaves, Indians from Calcutta and Chinese immigrants, totalling altogether about 2,500. The native inhabitants numbered 7,500, and were poor and disaffected.

Thus, the mercantile system prevailing at Bencoolen, though British, was the same as that put an end to in Java by Raffles. He immediately put an end to it here also. Forced cultivation of coffee and purchase of the crop at a low price were stopped. He also emancipated the slaves and ameliorated the lot of the transported felons by giving them land and encouraging them to marry and become settlers. Tribal rulers of the interior were invited to Government House and Raffles made friends with them. To make these changes widely known, he decided to tour the interior, though no roads existed, hardly even any paths; a vast forest, clothing range behind range of mountains, largely unexplored, stretched inland. That made touring the more attractive for him as a scientist. He set off before the end of April, taking Sophia with him, his botanist Arnold, fifty porters and an escort of six Malay soldiers, leaving Travers in charge at Bencoolen.

A letter of his dated 11 July to the Duchess of Somerset describes the first tour down the coast strip as far as a village called Manna, fifty miles from Bencoolen, and thence inland

The Rafflesia Arnoldi

to the mountains. Sophia was evidently a remarkable walker, for the marches sometimes lasted eight hours. When the track permitted they rode horses, seldom possible on account of the rocks and precipitous ascents. Of one march he has: 'The scenery was highly romantic and beautiful. During the night we were awakened by the approach of a party of elephants who seemed anxious to inquire our business in their domains; fortunately they kept some distance. . . . I must not omit to tell your Grace that in passing through the forest we were greatly annoyed by leeches; they got into our boots, which became filled with blood; at night too they fell off the leaves that sheltered us and in the morning we found ourselves bleeding profusely.' He goes on to tell her of an extraordinary flower which he came upon in the midst of the forest. 'It is perhaps the largest and most magnificent flower in the world.' It was a yard across, the nectary was a cup nine inches in diameter and nine in depth, capable of holding a gallon and a half of water. The whole plant weighed fifteen pounds. A model of it is to be seen today, prominently displayed, in the Victoria & Albert Museum, Natural History section. Its botanic name is Rafflesia Arnoldi, called so by Raffles as a memorial to his botanist, Arnold, to whom he was devoted and who died soon afterwards, the fatigue of the tour bringing on a fatal bout of malaria. The local name for the flower was the Devil's Betel Box. The colours were purple, yellow, white and brick-red, the substance of the petals thick and fleshy like a fungus. It had a horrible smell of carrion. This was Raffle's most singular botanic discovery. He found it impossible to take it with him, as it could not be preserved except in spirits, of which they carried nothing like enough. On a subsequent occasion, however, it appears that he was able to bring in a specimen.

The discovery of this unknown and extraordinary flower

was only one of the excitements of the tour. 'Lady Raffles,' he tells the Duchess, 'was a perfect heroine.' This was after a thirty mile march through thick forest and a night when their temporary shelter let in the pouring rain. In the more distant villages of the interior, where no white woman had ever been seen, she seemed to the inhabitants a supernatural being. In her *Memoir* she has: 'When the people first beheld me they seemed to be struck with amazement and the question was not, *who* is that? but, *what* is that?' Her clothes and the fairness of her complexion immediately suggested something out of this world. 'Mothers pressed in crowds, imploring to have their children touched as a preservative from all future evil.' It was useless for her to plead fatigue and ask to be excused. They demanded her magical touch. 'When one crowd was satisfied, another collected.' The number of children touched was very large. On one occasion she was resting by herself in a village hut with a sepoy sentry at the door to keep intruders off. 'But people collected in such numbers that they overpowered him, and hundreds rushed into the house to gaze. After this had been endured for some time they were entreated to retire' and let Sophia sleep. At this they all sat down and stared, saying there was nothing they would rather do than watch her going to sleep. It was impossible to get rid of them. At the next village there was the same eager worshipping crowd. They wanted to watch her eat this time and during the night she saw dark faces peeping through the curtain which surrounded her bed.

Sophia seems to have enjoyed being taken for a goddess. In the *Memoir* mention of herself is rare, and then always in the third person or as the editor. But this was a compliment she could not omit and one it was hard to think of Dutch women being paid.

There are other charming little glimpses of what it was

like a hundred and fifty years ago to travel through the forests of central Sumatra, where the trees were sometimes 200 feet high. Sophia records this: 'The porters came upon a tiger, crouched on the path; they immediately stopped and addressed him in terms of supplication, assuring him they were poor people carrying the Tuan Besar, great man's, luggage, who would be angry with them if they did not arrive in time. Therefore they implored permission to pass. The tiger . . . got up and walked quietly into the depths of the forest and they came on perfectly satisfied.' As Raffles explained in a letter to the Duchess, ancestral spirits were thought to reside in tigers and, though many were man-eaters, it was held disrespectful to resist them. 'When a tiger enters a village,' he writes, 'the people prepare rice and fruits as an offering.' The tiger, touched by their well-meant attentions, passes on.

During the tours Raffles made in May, June and July 1818, the chiefs of the various Sumatra tribes became attached to him, partly because his manner with them was so easy and pleasant, and also because he was abolishing practices which were oppressive. It is recorded that when he left their territories some of them wept to see him go. They were within the Dutch sphere and humbly asked for British protection. Heartened by their protestations, he had a vision of all Sumatra as a British dependency. The Dutch themselves, when they heard he was back in the East, began to have fears of this very thing. Perhaps he had been sent out for just that purpose. Should he succeed in suborning the principal rulers in Sumatra, the island might slip out of their grasp. His intrigues, as they called them, with one ruler in particular, the Sultan of Palembang, whose domain bordered the Straits of Sunda and so was on the doorstep of Java, especially alarmed them. They started a general tightening up of their relations with outlying sultans anywhere in the Archipelago, afraid that Raffles, by coming to an understanding with one or more of them, might secure for the British a trade settlement within the Dutch sphere and break their monopoly. As we know, the Dutch were quite right in suspecting him of this. He had his plans both for Sumatra, and beyond it. On his return from his tours in the interior he became aware that the Dutch were increasing their efforts to prevent British trespass in their preserves. The notion he already had formed while still in London that some settlement on an island in the Straits of Malacca was essential if British trade was to prosper, was now confirmed. Indeed, he would have to act quickly if he were to avoid the Dutch shutting him out by staking a claim to every suitable position. It was to this that in August 1818 he now applied himself. The tours had been interesting and informative, his administrative measures well advised. But he had come East again for more important reasons than the reform of administration in Bencoolen and natural history research. That the Dutch were watching him with apprehension, he knew. In one of his letters he wrote: 'They say I am a Spirit that will never allow the East to be quiet.'

Chapter Thirteen

RAFFLES RECEIVES THE SUPPORT OF HASTINGS

Marquess of Hastings invites Raffles to see him – his reasons for change of attitude – Raffles arrives at Calcutta with Sophia – Hastings's grandeur – discussions with him about the Straits – Hastings's instructions to Raffles, who is given powers to found a settlement – Raffles leaves Calcutta – calls at Penang – Governor of Penang's obstruction – Raffles sends Farquhar ahead to the Straits and follows him – they anchor off island of Singapore

S oon after Raffles's arrival in Bencoolen he had addressed the Governor General, the Marquess of Hastings (as Lord Moira had now become), and referring to the necessity of stopping the Dutch from reimposing their damaging trade restrictions, gave the view, which we know, that a British settlement on some island at the eastern end of the Straits of Malacca, would have that effect. As the authorities in London, he said, had instructed him to inquire into Dutch activities, he would welcome an opportunity of discussing matters with the Governor General.

The fact was that Raffles could take no action until he had Hastings's support. As they had not been on the best of terms in the past, he was delighted at the cordiality of Hastings's reply, which reached him in August 1818 on his return from one of his tours. The letter is so revealing that it requires full quotation. One should remember that Hastings and Raffles had so far never met.

July 6, 1818

Sir,

I have the honour to acknowledge your letter, and to offer my congratulations on your safe arrival.

It was painful to me, that I had, in the course of my public duty, to express an opinion unfavourable to certain of your measures in Java. The disapprobation, as you would perceive, affected their prudence alone; on the other hand no person can have felt more strongly than I did your anxious and unwearied exertions for ameliorating the condition of the native inhabitants under your sway. The procedure was no less recommended by wisdom than by benevolence; and the results have been highly creditable to the British Government.

I request you to consider yourself at liberty to carry into execution your wish of visiting Bengal, whensoever your convenience and the state of affairs in the Island may afford an eligible opportunity. . . .

Hastings would never have invited Raffles to a conference, did he not now view him in a light very different from formerly. Knighted by his bosom friend, the Regent, for his administration of Java and his researches into that island's history and resources, close friend of the late Princess Charlotte, whose admiration for him will have reached his ears, a figure in London high society, what a metamorphosis from the young Company officer who had been taken up by Minto, accused of corruption and incompetence by General Gillespie, and relieved of his post. The authorities, too, in London seemed from all accounts to have mellowed towards him, inasmuch as they had asked him to keep them posted on matters quite outside his normal duties in Bencoolen. Aware of all this, Hastings sought to make amends by the almost apologetic tone of his letter, pretending that he had never had anything against Raffles except a trifle about his imprudence, a very mild rendering of the fact that it was Hastings himself who had had him removed from his appointment as Lieutenant-Governor of Java. As has been suggested in his defence, Hastings had made at that time little study of affairs east of Calcutta, his whole attention being focussed westwards on the dire threat to the Company's domain in India by the Mahrattas and Pindaris. These adventurers he had lately routed, rescued central India from anarchy and given the inhabitants peace and security, services for which he had just received his Marquisate. With more leisure he had turned his attention eastwards, and after his brilliant victories was in no mood to sit still and watch the Dutch filch from the British lion what the creature had between its paws. Intelligence he had recently received about Dutch ambitions would have sufficed to make him anxious to hear what any Lieutenant-Governor of Bencoolen might have to say, and when that officer was the celebrity which Raffles had become, no wonder he wanted to meet him.

Raffles, always quick to seize an opportunity, immediately decided to set out for India. Ships were infrequent at Bencoolen and he had to avail himself of what came to hand. 'Sir Stamford,' writes Sophia, 'embarked on a very small vessel which had no better accommodation than one small cabin, with only a port-hole to admit air, where centipedes and scorpions roved about without interruption,' some kind of a trading brig owned by a country skipper, lacking, one supposes, a cabin with a window over the stern. Sophia accompanied him, leaving little Charlotte to be looked after by Mrs Grimes. It was the first week of September, the monsoon was at its height, and in the Bay of Bengal a mast went by the board. At the mouth of the Hugli, leading up to Calcutta, they took on a pilot, for the river was one of the most tricky in the East, the channel frequently changing. He got so drunk that in the middle of the night he ran them aground on a sandbank. There they stuck till rescue boats arrived from Calcutta, a hundred miles upstream. One may say that of all desolate spots to be stranded for some days, the mouth of the Hugli is one of the worst with the heat, mosquitoes, mud-coloured water and illimitable mangrove swamps beyond.

On 29 September Raffles landed at Calcutta, receiving the salute of guns due to a Lieutenant-Governor. It is not on record whether he stayed at Government House, though where else he could have stayed is difficult to guess. In a letter to the Duchess of Somerset dated 26 November he writes: 'I have begged Lady Raffles to give your Grace an account of the *regal state* of the Governor General, which really exceeds all I had heard of it.' Hastings considered that Lord Minto's style had been too modest and modelled himself on the splendid Marquess Wellesley. His household establishment resembled that of royalty; he had a chamberlain on a salary of £3,000 a year. His wife, Countess of Loudoun, last mentioned at St Helena on her way home in April 1816, when Napoleon considered it an impertinence to be asked to meet her, had just arrived back in Calcutta. Her practice at receptions was to enter with her train held up by pages, and be conducted into the dining room ahead of her guests. Since her husband's promotion in the peerage she had adopted the style of Marchioness of Hastings. When Hastings went out driving it was in a carriage and four, an open barouche, with grooms running beside each horse and half a dozen macebearers running in front, the very outfit Minto could not stand. At a reception he liked to use a sword said to have been carried at Agincourt, though it is hard to believe that story, as such a sword would have been too heavy. But stiff and disinclined though he was to go informally among his guests, or speak familiarly with any person, he was not disagreeable to do business with, was never off-hand, for the tone he assumed was correct in a grand manner and not displeasing. As he had come out from home heavily in debt, clearly he was not saving a penny.

Raffles had no difficulty in getting on with this English aristocrat cast in the rôle of oriental despot. It transpired that Hastings had received advices from the Governor of Penang adducing evidence, similar to Raffles's, of Dutch intransigence and urging the founding of a strong point much nearer the eastern exit of the Straits than was Penang. Raffles had never found that his views coincided with those of the Penang government, but on this occasion the logic of events brought this about. It may be recalled that in 1811, when Minto and Raffles were at Malacca before the invasion of Java, the Resident of Malacca was William Farquhar. At the rendition of the Dutch empire Malacca had been restored to Holland with the rest. As the merchant community of Penang feared that the Dutch would develop Malacca to the detriment of Penang's trade, and from there would get a stranglehold on the China route, they pressed Colonel Bannerman, the Governor, to send Farquhar to explore the groups of islands off the end of the Malay peninsula at the eastern exit of the Straits and report whether a British settlement could be made on any one of them to offset the return of Malacca. This he did in July 1816, two years before the present meeting of Raffles and Hastings. The islands belonged to the mainland Malay state of Johore, the succession to whose throne was in dispute. Farquhar thought that one of the island groups called the Carimons, twenty miles south of Singapore, would be the most suitable for the settlement in view. He reported this to Colonel Bannerman, who took no action beyond writing off to inform the Governor General in Council. All this had happened when Raffles was in England. While there, he heard of Farquhar's reconnaissance and in his memorandum for George Canning made use of that knowledge. On reaching Bencoolen he took up the project himself, and as stated wrote to Hastings. Now, in his discussions with him, the fact that the commercial community of Penang desired a Straits settlement gave weight to what he was advocating.

The talks with Hastings went well. On 16 October, about a fortnight after arrival at Calcutta, Raffles was able to write to Marsden, his friend and confidant in London: 'You will be happy to hear that I have made my peace with the Marquess of Hastings . . . I am now struggling hard to interest this Supreme Government in the Eastern Islands.' He goes on to declare, however, that he thinks Hastings will have to make a reference to London before he can authorize him to go ahead. That would mean considerable delay. But the matter is urgent, he tells Marsden. 'Every day, every hour, that the Dutch are left to themselves, their influence increases and our difficulties will be proportionately increased.' He is referring in particular to the pressure the Dutch were bringing to bear on all sultans not to make agreements of any kind with the British. A settlement, he says, can only be effected by agreement with some sultan. If the British do not take action at once there will be no place left in the Straits. The Dutch will have anticipated them everywhere. Hastings, however, was reluctant to rush into any course antipathetic to the Dutch. His instructions from London on that point were emphatic. There was an element, however, of bluster in Dutch policy which he did not like at all. They had, he felt, a very poor case. They were Britain's ally, who had done them proud, first delivering them from the French in the East, and, after overthrowing Napoleon in the West, handing them back their island empire, and restoring their homeland as a power. Yet now here they were making claims beyond anything they had enjoyed before. They had no shadow of right in his opinion to threaten British communications with China; and to refuse a limited free trade within the Dutch sphere, even a trade with outlying sultans, was an extremely illiberal attitude towards a nation to which they were so much in debt. Nevertheless, the mood of the Court and Board in London was such that he was given no latitude. He was to let things be. It was an extraordinary lack of foresight. The Dutch were well aware of the British government's supineness and proposed to take as much advantage of it as they could. It encouraged them to make a fuss about trifles, to protest to Hastings against Raffles's doings in Bencoolen. He had overstepped the mark, particularly in the case of the sultanate of Palembang, and was tempting here, there and everywhere, they said, Sumatran chiefs to throw off Dutch allegiance. There was some truth in this, for in fact such was Raffles's intention. So far, however, he had done no damage, but they wanted him called to order before he did. They were genuinely afraid of him.

However, Hastings was a big man and, having begun to see the sense of things, he decided to take the responsibility of a move, in spite of the expressed wishes of the London authorities. What Raffles wanted from him was leave to slip into one of the islands in the Straits, an island which the Dutch had not so far declared to be in their zone, and fix a settlement. Let them complain afterwards, he urged. They would have no case. And as they would know their case was bad, they would do no more than bluster for a while and give way in the end. Their pretensions were preposterous. What could they do? Fight the British fleet! That was the right way to handle Hastings, fresh from his victories. He was won over. To throw the Dutch off the scent he wrote disavowing what they alleged Raffles had done in Sumatra, but gave him the backing he required in the main project of a Straits settlement.

His instructions to Raffles are dated 28 November 1818. They give the impression of being founded on a draft written by Raffles himself. The letter begins by saying that Hastings is confiding to his management the Straits affair, an undertaking outside his duties as Lieutenant-Governor of Bencoolen. There is no doubt, he goes on, that the Dutch intend to extend their supremacy over the whole of the Eastern Seas by possessing themselves of all the commanding stations in that quarter. The success of this project would have the effect of completely excluding British shipping from the Archipelago except on such terms as the Dutch might impose, such as high customs charges, and would give them entire command of the only two channels for the trade between China and Europe, undesirable in peace, intolerable in case of hostilities. The restitution of the Islands to Holland after the European war gave that country control of the Straits of Sunda, one of the approaches to the China Seas; the other approach, the Straits of Malacca, must be secured for the free passage of British commerce, to be effected by the establishment of a station commanding the eastern entrance to the Straits.

So far the letter recapitulates exactly what Raffles had been advocating. It goes on to indicate where the station should be located. Reference is made to the islands already investigated by Farquhar. There are three groups lying adjacent to each other in the mouth of the Straits, Rhio, Linga and the Carimons. Rhio, says the letter, is perhaps the best suited for the purpose. As far as is known, the Dutch have not extended their supremacy over its ruling sultan, who when Farquhar was there seemed inclined to enter into engagements with the British. Raffles should ascertain whether such is the position at the moment. An agreement with the sultan to establish a mere trading post there will not be sufficient, for, when the Dutch learn what has taken place, they may oblige the sultan to acknowledge their supremacy, and disclaim all agreements he may have made with the British. The settlement will have to be defended by a military force strong enough to discourage the Dutch from attempting to seize it. In the event, therefore, of the Dutch not having already occupied Rhio, measures should immediately be taken 'for permanently establishing British interests at that port and his Lordship is pleased to confide the negotiations and arrangements to your judgment and discretion'. Raffles's experience in those parts makes it unnecessary to give him more specific instructions. Farquhar is to accompany him and be left in charge of the settlement. Whatever troops and stores may be necessary are to be supplied by the Governor of Penang, Colonel Bannerman. Farquhar, however, will not be subordinate to that authority, but to Raffles as Lieutenant-Governor of Bencoolen. A frigate will be placed at his disposal. Colonel Bannerman has been sent orders to give him full support.

The letter adds that if it should turn out that the Dutch have already established themselves at Rhio, Raffles will, of course, 'abstain from all negotiation and collision'. He should now leave at once on board the frigate allotted to him, call at Penang, obtain from Bannerman the troops required, and then proceed to the Straits.

These instructions gave Raffles a completely free hand provided Rhio was available. But since Hastings insisted that a settlement was essential, the presumption was that if Rhio was not available some other locality should be sought. Raffles was thus given *carte blanche,* or so he considered, for he intended to interpret his orders so widely that they could be made to cover whatever he himself decided to do. He wrote to the Duchess of Somerset: 'I have full powers to do all we can; and if anything is to be done, I think I need not assure your Grace that it shall be done – and quickly done.' That was the point. The authorities in Bengal had been so supine in allowing the Dutch their head, that he might be too late. But he would manage it somehow. He sailed on 7 December 1818. Two days before he left, however, it occurred to Hastings to supplement his letter of 28 November by advising him to try Johore, the state at the tip of the Malay peninsula, in the event of Rhio not being available. If on inquiry Johore seemed satisfactory 'you will be pleased to open negotiations with the Chief of Johore, and carry into effect at that place an arrangement similar to the one at present contemplated for Rhio.' Hastings also wrote a soothing letter to the Court in London, reporting what he had done, but in such vague terms as not to arouse apprehension.

On 12 December, anchored at the mouth of the Hugli, Raffles wrote to Marsden, his confidant. The letter shows what solution was uppermost in his mind. 'We are now on our way to the Eastward in the hope of doing something, but I much fear the Dutch have hardly left us an inch of ground to stand upon. My attention is principally directed to Johore and you must not be surprised if my next letter to you is dated from the site of the ancient city of Singapura.' Raffles was off to Singapore, the place that for long he himself had thought more suitable than Rhio or the Carimons.

He arrived at Penang on the last day of 1818 in time to dine with Bannerman that evening at Suffolk House, the

EASTERN ENTRANCE TO THE STRAITS OF MALACCA

Governor's handsome residence. The news was disconcerting. The Dutch, having guessed what was in the wind, had occupied Rhio. Bannerman, though he had pressed for the establishment of a settlement in the Straits, disliked Raffles so much and was so jealous of him that he was happy to see him baulked and said that he supposed in the circumstances his trip eastwards was off. Till he got Hastings's orders to supply Raffles with troops and lend him all assistance, he had seen himself as the man who was going to found the Straits settlement with the help of Farquhar. He now hoped that the Dutch occupation of Rhio would lead to a long postponement, since a reference to Calcutta and London would be necessary. Raffles would have to go back to Bencoolen. But in the supplementary instructions which Raffles had received from Hastings he was clearly authorized, if Rhio were not available, to try Johore without further reference. This he deemed ample sanction to proceed with his mission. He informed Bannerman of this some days later, stating that Farquhar agreed and was ready to accompany him in accordance with the Governor General's directive. Bannerman adduced further specious arguments why Raffles should desist and wrote to Hastings to that effect. Raffles paid no attention to him, but hurried on with his preparations to sail eastwards within a fortnight. Bannerman sought to prevent him going and raised such difficulties that Raffles became anxious. On 16 January 1819 he wrote to Marsden complaining bitterly of Bannerman's obstruction. 'But I will persevere steadily in what I conceive to be my duty. I think I may rely on the Marquess, his last words to me were – "Sir Stamford, you may depend on me".'

If Raffles had not had to look to Bannerman to supply the troops, he could, on the strength of his orders from the Marquess, have sailed on, disregarding what this stupid and malicious Colonel might attempt. As it was he had to outwit him. The way he did it was ingenious. On 16 January 1819, a fortnight after his arrival, he sent Farquhar with Bannerman's knowledge eastward into the Straits with the frigate and some other small ships, ostensibly on a further reconnaissance and survey of the islands near Singapore. Bannerman was persuaded to let him take a few soldiers with him. It was given out that Raffles would wait in Penang until an answer from Hastings was received to Bannerman's representation that no attempt to found a settlement be made at the moment. Farquhar set sail as directed but had to anchor his little fleet outside Penang harbour to wait for the tide. Raffles sent a boat out with a message that he would be following the next day in a merchant ship, the *Indiana*, which, unnoticed by Bannerman, he had kept lying by. During the night the *Indiana* was got ready and he embarked at daybreak, leaving a note for Bannerman, to be delivered when his ship was under the horizon, to say that he had thought it prudent to oversee Farquhar's activities. He did not overtake Farquhar for ten days, by which time (27 January 1819) his ships were lying off the Carimon islands. The previous day he had had a look at them, for they were the place he most favoured for a settlement, though others disagreed. On Raffles joining him in the *Indiana*, orders were given to make sail for the island of Singapore. There the ships anchored off a fine sandy beach at 4 p.m. on 28 January 1819.

Chapter Fourteen

RAFFLES FOUNDS SINGAPORE

The founding of Singapore – Description of the island – the former city – Raffles lands – meets the Temenggong – sends for Tunku Long, the legitimate heir of Johore – installs him as Sultan – Agreement drawn up – The settlement planned – Raffles places Farquhar in charge and leaves

The island of Singapore is twenty-six miles from west to east and fourteen from north to south, and is thus only very slightly larger than the Isle of Wight. A strait about a quarter of a mile wide at its narrowest divides it from the mainland, which here is the Malay state of Johore. It is as much a part of Johore as is the Isle of Wight of England. In 1819 there was nothing remarkable about its appearance. It was mostly flat, with a low hill here and there, swampy, densely wooded and sparsely inhabited. For hundreds of years ships to and from Canton had passed close to it, a familiar, but not interesting, sight. A walled city belonging to the empire of Sri Vijaya, a great Hindu-Buddhist state, had stood there until the break up of that empire towards the end of the fourteenth century. Nothing had ever been built on it since. Malacca had taken its place as the entrepôt of the Straits. The Sanscritic name of the old city was Singhapura, the Lion City, that is the holy city of the Lord Vishnu. It is interesting to recall that Marco Polo, who passed through the

Straits about the year 1284, very probably saw the ancient city, for he landed at Rhio.

As soon as Raffles was anchored, some of the island's inhabitants came aboard. He was glad to know from them that the Dutch had never landed there; Rhio, twenty miles away, was the nearest they had been. He said he wished to call on the chief of the place and sent a message ashore to that effect. The chief was styled the Temenggong; he was a prince of the house of Johore.

On landing next morning, the 29 January 1819, Raffles accompanied by Farquhar and one sepoy went straight to the Temenggong's house, the largest in the little village above the beach, some of whose inhabitants seemed to be sea gypsies, a wandering Malay tribe who preferred boats to houses, and made a living as pearlers and pirates. The Temenggong gave the Englishmen a cordial reception. Raffles did not delay in coming to the point. The British would like to make a settlement on Singapore island. As it had an excellent harbour and was right on the course taken by ships through the Straits, it would make a good entrepôt between Canton and Calcutta. The resulting trade would benefit the local inhabitants as well as the British. If the Temenggong granted a lease, he would be offered an attractive rent. The Temenggong replied that he would be glad to do so, but that the matter did not rest with him. Singapore island belonged to Johore, as did the Rhio, Linga and Carimon groups of islands. The consent of the Sultan of Johore would have to be obtained.

Raffles, of course, knew this very well. He also knew that the succession to the throne of Johore was in dispute. The Sultan had died six years before, leaving two sons. The elder, Tunku Long, had been designated as his successor. But Tunku Long was not on the spot at the moment of his father's death, and by the time he got back to Johore he found that his younger brother, who had been acting as regent during his absence, refused to step down at the instigation of his uncle, who lived in Rhio, of which he was ruler. Raffles had plans to turn this disputed succession to his advantage. The usurper, who lived in the Linga group, had received Dutch recognition. If Raffles supported the legitimate heir and obtained from him the concession he required, he would be out-manoeuvring the Dutch. Tunku Long was not at Singapore. He was on a small island called Bulang in the Rhio group. Thus the Johore royal family was scattered among the state's islands – the usurping brother in Linga, the uncle in Rhio, the Temenggong in Singapore and the rightful heir in Bulang. The Dutch had just taken over both the Rhio and the Linga group, but had left Singapore. In all this Raffles saw his chance. He would send for Tunku Long, the legitimate heir, proclaim him Sultan and get him to grant the concession. A messenger was despatched at once to bring him from Bulang 'by hook or by crook even if he had only one shirt on his back', as Abdullah puts it in his memoir, the *Hikayat*.

Pending his arrival, Raffles persuaded the Temenggong to make a preliminary agreement, to be endorsed later when Tunku Long turned up, authorizing him to bring his men ashore at once and establish the post. The soldiers, about a company of sepoys, were landed with the baggage. Tents were pitched and a mat house erected for Raffles. On rising ground at the back of the village he selected a site for a fort and ordered work to begin straight away. Twelve guns were brought ashore to a bastion by the sea. It was a tiny force with which to bring off the greatest political and commercial *coup* of the century. Clive at Plassey founded the British Empire in India with 900 European soldiers and 2,100 sepoys. But Raffles had not more than 340 sepoys and 100 sailors.

Two days later, 31 January, he wrote to Marsden: 'Here I

am at Singapore, true to my word. Most certainly the Dutch never had a Factory in the island.' That they had taken over Rhio and Linga and made agreements with the usurping sultan 'ought not to interfere with our permanent establishment here'.

Tunku Long arrived next day, 1 February. He had not a prepossessing appearance and was hesitant when he realized it was Raffles's intention to make him Sultan of Johore; what would happen when the Dutch found out? Raffles set to work to talk him over, 'smiling with infinite charm . . . his words sweet as a sea of honey. . . . The very stones would have melted on hearing his words'. Thus Abdullah, in translation from his flowery Malay. When the Temenggong and another important prince of Johore added their solicitations, Tunku Long found courage and agreed to take the throne. Indeed, he became so animated by the prospect that he suggested, to make a good job of it, a massacre of all the Dutch in Rhio. Here Raffles had to restrain him; he was evidently more of a savage than desirable, if he were to be represented as a poor fellow done out of his rights. However, the thing had to be fixed that way. An installation ceremony was arranged for 6 February. This was made as imposing as possible. The ships were decked with flags, the officers landed in full uniform, about thirty of them, and provided Raffles with a tolerable suite. The troops were drawn up. Three chairs, the biggest for Raffles, the other two for Farquhar and the new Sultan, were placed in one of the tents, a red carpet of broadcloth leading to the door. At 1 p.m. Raffles stood to receive the Sultan at the entrance. Escorted by a guard of Malays, Tunku Long walked up the carpet between lines of Sepoys at the present. Raffles conducted him to his chair. A crowd of Malays and Chinese assembled to look on. The treaty which Raffles had drawn up was then read and signed by him, as Agent of the Governor General. The Sultan's seal was attached. Presents were then distributed, opium and arms. Tunku Long made a bad impression on some of the English present, because he was sweating so profusely. But that was a small matter; the *coup* had come off. He was Sultan, his grant had the force of law. After the ceremony, the Union Jack was hoisted and salutes were fired by the sepoys and artillery. The Europeans, accompanied by the principal Malays, then adjourned to where drinks were laid out. Toast after toast was drunk, making everyone very lively. The party broke up at 4 p.m. The occasion was hardly comparable to a reception at Carlton House, but seemed very brilliant in the bamboo village of Singapore, where nothing like it had happened for four hundred years.

The terms of the treaty may be stated shortly. In return for the right granted to the East India Company to maintain a settlement, Tunku Long was to get 5,000 Spanish dollars annually and be protected by the British against outside interference. The grant of 3,000 dollars annually to the Temenggong, offered the week before, was confirmed. As long as the British maintained the settlement, the Sultan undertook not to let any other nation in, and to resist by force an attempt by intruders. The administration would be conducted by the British, who would bear all expenses.

In addition Raffles published a proclamation in which Farquhar was declared Resident and Commandant, and all persons were enjoined to obey him. He would be under the authority of the Lieutenant-Governor of Bencoolen, and was to exercise the greatest care not to interfere in any place where the Dutch had established their authority, nor ever publicly to criticize their actions, no matter what his opinion of them. In the case of states, however, not yet fallen under their authority, he should preserve a helpful attitude, ready to oblige them, for instance, with arms to maintain their independence, as this would increase British influence in the eastern seas, as should properly be the result of the founding of Singapore. Raffles also made arrangement for staff. A Secretary and a Master Attendant of the Port were appointed, their pay at 400 and 300 dollars per month, sums to be compared with Raffles's own pay in 1805 as Assistant Secretary to the Penang government when he drew 500 dollars.

Farquhar was further instructed to organize convenient watering places for passing vessels, as at river mouths with firm shingle for rolling the casks. No customs dues were to be levied; Singapore was to be a free port. He was to get on at once with the fort on the rise. It should be designed so that ten-pounder guns could be mounted, and be large enough to accommodate thirty European artillerymen and the rest of the garrison in an emergency. In addition the Settlement's flanks should be protected by strong batteries, and a Martello tower erected, which, entrenchments and palisades, should suffice to render the Settlement secure. As this military aspect of his duties was of great importance, Farquhar was to have as assistant a lieutenant of the Bengal Artillery, whose pay was fixed at 200 dollars a month. Further troops would be required and would be sent. Raffles concludes by discussing the building of a house for Farquhar and making rules for accounts.

We may justly marvel at his capacity to find the time and concentration to draw up such minute instructions when engaged on so hazardous an adventure, and also at the confidence in the future which his orders display. He was aware that what he had done might be disallowed by the higher authorities, for he had certainly interpreted their advices very freely, so freely, indeed, that he had gone far beyond anything contemplated in Calcutta. Hastings never dreamed of his taking so independent a line as to put his own man on the throne of Johore in the sudden way it was done. Nevertheless, he was as calm and collected as if drafting despatches in a secretariat, and what he writes gives a finished and orderly touch to proceedings of the utmost boldness. Yet he was not without momentary anxieties. There were occasions when doubts assailed him, for he wrote to his Duchess: 'If this last effort to secure our interests fails, I must quit politics and turn philosopher.' He left Singapore on 7 February. The whole business had only taken a week.

Chapter Fifteen

HASTINGS STANDS BY RAFFLES

Raffles's independence compared with Nelson's — Raffles knew Dutch must object to Singapore settlement, but risked it — Bannerman refuses to send reinforcements — Reaction at Malacca — Tunku Long writes — Bannerman tries to baulk Raffles by denouncing him to Hastings — Capellen asks Hastings to disavow Raffles's settlement at Singapore — Tunku Long retracts — Raffles visits Achin — Commercial opinion in Calcutta supports Raffles — Hastings writes a scorching letter to Bannerman and orders him to send reinforcements — Sophia's second child born at Penang — Raffles returns to Singapore and finds it growing fast — Hopes of receiving Court's sanction — Raffles lays out Singapore — returns to Bencoolen

It has been said of Nelson that, after the battle of the Nile in 1798, which stopped the French from marching on India, he became incapable of acting as a subordinate, the most famous example of his independence being in 1801 at the battle of Copenhagen when, as second in command to Admiral Sir Hyde Parker, he disobeyed that weak man's order to disengage, put his telescope to his blind eye in playful mockery and drove on to victory. Raffles's mood at Singapore was analogous. He had talked the Marquess of Hastings — a bigger man certainly than the nonentity, Sir Hyde Parker — into agreeing that a station in the Straits was essential and into giving him, with many reservations, authority to find and settle such a place, provided he did not risk a collision with the Dutch. But that was precisely the risk he did take. Johore consisted of the whole end of the Malay peninsula, together with the three archipelagos off its southern tip, the Carimon, Rhio and Linga. The Dutch view was that in virtue of their possession of Malacca, returned to them in the 1816 rendition of their islands, the whole of Johore was within their sphere and always had been, inasmuch as it lay between Malacca and the great Islands. In short, their claim was that the eastern mouth of the Straits of Malacca fell by force of geography within their eastern empire. This was a necessary corollary of their *mare clausum* policy. The gates to their monopolies were the straits of Malacca and Sunda. For the British to put a fortified post at the strategic centre of the former was an intrusion of the most provoking kind. Raffles knew they were bound to protest, but gambled on their not using force to evict him. If Hastings continued to back him, London would come round when the importance of what he had achieved was fully realized. It would then be a matter of negotiation with the Dutch, who would have to come to terms. But the affair was not going to pass off as smoothly as that. There were to be some agitating moments first. He wrote to Marsden: 'I have a violent opposition to surmount on the part of the Government of Penang.' He had Bannerman, a jealous, malicious, angry man to cope with. True, he was not under Bannerman's orders, but it was within Bannerman's power to make things very unpleasant.

When Raffles left Singapore on 7 February 1819, he did not go on to Bencoolen and resume his duties there, but returned to Penang which he reached on 13 February. He immediately sent a letter to the Chief Secretary to the

Governor General, detailing what had taken place at Singapore, declaring he was satisfied that the British title to the island was sound, as Tunku Long was beyond question the legitimate heir to Johore, and declaring that the foundation would suffice 'to prevent the reappearance of the system of exclusive monopoly which the Dutch once exercised in these seas and would willingly re-establish'. Malacca was by-passed; England now commanded the gateway to China and the eastern seas.

That letter sent, he had to face Bannerman. Some events then occurred which strengthened Bannerman's hand. Two captains of British ships were in Malacca when the Singapore news came in. They learned that the Dutch governor there was so furious that he swore he would embark at once for Singapore and bring back Farquhar in chains. Some days later the captains reported this at Penang to Bannerman. News also came in that Tunku Long and the Temenggong, as soon as Raffles left, lost their nerve and wrote to the Governor of Malacca and to their rivals, the other brother and the uncle in Rhio, saying that Raffles had forced them to yield him Singapore by threats. Bannerman, already very sour at the way Raffles had slipped out of Penang and surreptitiously founded Singapore, was now convinced that his view of the imprudence of such a move was confirmed. When Raffles let him have a copy of his letter to the Indian government and followed this by a request that two hundred more soldiers be sent to Singapore to discourage any violent reaction by the Dutch, Bannerman refused to send a single man. This refusal he reported to Hastings in a letter where he tried to ridicule and discredit Raffles. Why, said he, the British title to Singapore island is worthless, for Tunku Long was not the legitimate heir. The whole affair is an example of Raffles's ambition run wild. And what nonsense, anyway, to put Singapore under Bencoolen! It is eight weeks sail from there, but only eight days from Penang. It ought to be under me, not him.

A few days later, 16 February, the Dutch official protest was received in Penang. The Governor General of Java, Baron van der Capellen, was under the impression that, as soon as the Marquess of Hastings heard what had happened, he would repudiate Raffles's coup. He was misled by the letter mentioned further back, which Hastings had written him, saying that Raffles had exceeded his instructions in Sumatra, when he sought to detach the Sultan of Palembang from his Dutch allegiance. Bannerman sent Capellen's protest on to Hastings, and wrote a note to Raffles advising him to order Farquhar to evacuate Singapore, as a collision with the Dutch was probable if he did not.

In the face of this attempt to damage him, Raffles remained calm and refrained from entering into an altercation with a man for whom he felt nothing but contempt, a man whose timidity was matched by his lack of grasp and his judgment clouded by jealousy. It remained to be seen, however, how his aspersions would be received in Calcutta. Would Hastings keep his word and stand by Raffles, or would he desert him?

It can be said, I think, that if Capellen had been as daring a man as Raffles and had sent immediately men and ships to Singapore, he could have forced Farquhar to clear out, though Farquhar had declared that he would make a fight for it with his 340 soldiers and ten guns. And if Capellen had taken Singapore, Hastings would have been forbidden by the Court to send a force to take it back. Singapore would have been lost. But Capellen had not the daring. Besides, he told himself, a diplomatic letter would suffice. He wrote accordingly to Hastings, adopting the confident tone of a man who had only to state his case to win it. Before 1795, he said, the year that the British first took Malacca from the Dutch, Johore was a dependency of Malacca and Singapore was part of Johore. With the return of Malacca to the Dutch in 1816, Johore automatically became its dependency again. By taking Singapore, Raffles had seized a part of the Dutch empire. He was sure his Lordship would disavow so high-handed an action and restore Singapore to its legal owners.

Hearing that the Dutch were putting their faith in negotiation and that there was no fear of an attack on Singapore, Tunku Long and the Temenggong took courage and wrote in to say that Raffles had, in fact, not forced them. They had let him settle, as they had full right to do, since Tunku Long was the legitimate heir and had succeeded to the throne in a legitimate manner.

Raffles had arrived at Penang, as we have seen, on 13 February 1819; now on 8 March he left for Achin, the Moslem sultanate at the top end of Sumatra. As his mission there was of minor importance, it will suffice to record that it had to do with a disputed succession. Achin was situated on the western entrance to the Straits, and Raffles had Hastings's instructions to support the man likely to be of most use to the East India Company. Though the Dutch aspired to exercise an overlordship throughout Sumatra, they had no hold on Achin nor were in a hurry to assert one, as it lay some 1,000 miles outside their *mare clausum*. Raffles's visit was hardly noticed by them, particularly as their attention was fixed on what was happening at Singapore. He was back in Penang on 28 April. During his absence of nearly two months the Singapore drama had continued to unfold.

Bannerman had sent another despatch to Hastings, enclosing the letters from Tunku Long and the Temenggong in which they retracted their allegation that Raffles had forced them. The letters, wrote Bannerman, merely showed that the

retraction had been forced by Farquhar. He repeated that
Tunku Long's title was worthless. If he was the legitimate
sultan why did he write timidly to his Rhio uncle asking to
be forgiven? As for Singapore, Bannerman went on, it could
not be defended against forces the Dutch could bring against
it. To reinforce it would be merely to throw away men, and
he was not sending any. Raffles was responsible for the com-
bustion which threatened Farquhar and had left him to get
out as best he could, like a man who sets fire to a house and
himself runs for his life.

On 19 March, eleven days after Raffles left for Achin, the
controversy took a turn in Calcutta which was to have
decisive effect. The occupation of Singapore and the treaty
which Raffles had made with Tunku Long on 6 February
were reported in the Calcutta press. An article in the *Calcutta
Journal*, the chief mouthpiece of commercial opinion, declared
the founding of Singapore an event of the greatest moment
for the China trade, for which it would act as a fulcrum. The
hope was expressed that the settlement would receive the
fullest support of the government. Hastings was congratu-
lated for his part in ending the Dutch attempt to re-establish
a trade monopoly in eastern seas.

These and other plaudits in the press greatly strengthened
Hastings. By 16 March he had received Raffles's full account
of the founding of Singapore, sent off from Penang about
15 February. On first reading the despatch he had been somewhat startled. Raffles had stretched his instructions very far.
He had risked collision with the Dutch, a collision which, if
it caused no more than a diplomatic hubbub, was bad
enough, but which if it resulted in fighting would bring
down a stern rebuke from the Court. Now, however, with
commercial Calcutta's favourable reaction, he felt able to
write Raffles a letter supporting him. It contained the follow-

ing sentences: 'The selection of Singapore is considered highly judicious and your proceedings in establishing a Factory there do honour to your approved skill and ability, though the measure itself as incurring a collision with the Dutch authorities is to be regretted. . . . Your engagement with the presumed legitimate Chief of Johore and the local Government of Singapore are provisionally confirmed. . . . It is intended to maintain the Post of Singapore for the present.'

So Hastings kept his promise. But the storm was not over, for London had not spoken yet. His correspondence with the Court would be very delicate. And he must soothe Capellen. But he wrote Bannerman a scorching letter, whose meddling, he now saw, had encouraged the Dutch and made things worse. The more he thought of it, the more insolent seemed Bannerman's behaviour. He himself might have to submit to censure from above; he was certainly not going to stand impertinence from below. It was not your business, he told the Colonel, to give any opinion on Sir Stamford Raffles's proceedings and certainly not to criticize them. All you were ordered to do was to help him. But you took it upon yourself to refuse him troops. If through your disobedience to orders the Dutch are tempted to violence by the weakness of the military force at Singapore 'we fear you will have difficulty in excusing yourself'. Let him at once send reinforcing troops.

Bannerman grovelled on receiving this letter. On 18 May he replied that he had 'received a lesson which would teach him how again to presume to offer opinions as long as he lived'. He begged Hastings to believe that his intentions had been well meant. He had never quarrelled with Sir Stamford. 'On the contrary he and his amiable Lady have received from me since their first arrival from Calcutta every personal

civility and attention which Your Excellency had desired me
to show them. . . . Malicious revenge I thank God my heart
knows not and never has known.' After despatching this letter
he immediately sent two hundred men and six thousand
rupees to Singapore. Three months later he died of cholera.

Raffles had left Sophia in Penang while away. By the time
he was back from Achin her second child, a boy, was born.
He was given the name Leopold, after Prince Leopold of
Saxe-Coburg. Writing shortly afterwards to Colonel Adden-
brooke, late Equerry to the Princess Charlotte, he told him
how he had called his two children Leopold and Charlotte
so that those two names 'ever dear and ever respected' may
continually be on his lips. He, Sophia and the baby left
Penang on 22 May *en route* for Bencoolen via Singapore, as
he wished to call there and see how his new town had come
on since he left it in February. They got there on 31 May
and stayed three weeks. In a long letter to Colonel Adden-
brooke, for whom he had a warm friendship since the time
he used to visit the Princess Charlotte at Claremont, he wrote
how wonderfully Singapore had developed in three and a
half months. 'Already a population of about five thousand
souls has collected under our flag. . . . The harbour is filled
with shipping from all quarters. . . . Everyone is comfort-
ably housed, provisions are in abundance, the troops healthy.'
The inhabitants were chiefly Chinese who had moved in
from Malacca and Rhio. Raffles also wrote to other influential
friends in London, such as his regular correspondent, the
Duchess of Somerset, and to Sir Robert Inglis, one of the
directors of the East India Company, a supporter of his, who
would, he knew, strive to persuade the other directors that
Singapore must be retained. 'All we want now is the certainty
of permanent possession, and this, of course, depends on
authorities beyond our control', he writes in another letter,

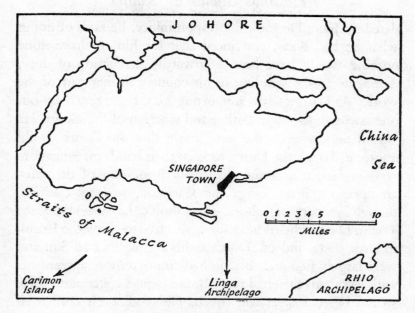

SINGAPORE ISLAND

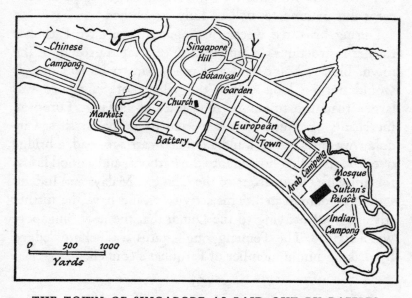

THE TOWN OF SINGAPORE AS LAID OUT BY RAFFLES

dated 15 June. He took the responsibility, he said, of doing what he had done, convinced that for him to have done nothing would have been a cowardly dereliction of duty, damaging to the standing of his country in that part of the world. As Hastings was supporting him, there remained but one essential, the approbation and sanction of the Court. He would persevere on the assumption that the Court would approve. To ask the Dutch to keep their hands off Singapore was, in fact, a minimum demand. Possession of the three archipelagos, Rhio, Linga and Carimon, was not claimed, though, as part of Johore, they should be surrendered to Tunku Long, who, if he desired, was free to allow the British to settle there. Indeed, Dutch rights throughout all Sumatra were largely fictional. Britain had come to more agreements with its sultans than had they. But to expect concessions there would be to expect too much. He would rest content if Britain took her stand on the retention of Singapore. 'If I keep Singapore I shall be quite satisfied,' he tells Marsden. 'In a few years our influence over the Archipelago, as far as concerns our commerce, will be fully established.'

During his three weeks in Singapore, he gave Farquhar further instructions. In anticipation of a rapid growth of the town, blocks, house sites and roads had to be laid out. It would not be long before the village of Singapore was larger than the towns of Malacca and Penang. European merchants of repute were expected to apply for sites. Farquhar was ordered to build a circular carriage road, a bridge over the river that flowed into the harbour, and a good house for himself. The quarters of the Chinese, Malays and Indians should be demarcated. This activity would have the further advantage of proving to the Dutch that the new Singapore was a fixture. The Temenggong's status was acknowledged by making him a member of Farquhar's council.

Raffles's Return to Bencoolen

Raffles and his party left for Bencoolen on 28 June 1819. Sophia in her *Memoir* has this anecdote of the voyage, which was via the Straits of Sunda: 'The only event was the vessel striking on a bank in the Straits of Rhio during the night. It was feared that she would not be got off and a small boat was prepared' to take Raffles and the family back to Singapore. Just as they were about to abandon the vessel, someone suggested that emptying the water-casks overboard would lighten the ship enough for her to float clear of the bank. This worked and they continued on their way. On getting abreast of a Dutch settlement on Rhio, a boat was sent ashore to ask for a refill of the casks. 'The Dutch Resident refused all intercourse.' This must have been because he heard that Raffles was on board. Fortunately an American clipper came in sight. 'The Captain generously stopped his course and with great difficulty by means of ropes conveyed some casks of water.' The voyage continued through the Sunda straits, 'a scene of enchantment', and round to Bencoolen, which was reached on 31 July.

Chapter Sixteen

CONTROVERSY OVER SINGAPORE

Raffles waits at Bencoolen for London reaction to foundation of Singapore – writes to Wilberforce describing how he seeks to improve lot of people and asks for his support – Raffles both a statesman and a forerunner of future developments in Asia – Domestic details – Sophia left in Bencoolen when Raffles sails for Calcutta to see Hastings – finds Hastings optimistic about Singapore and traders enthusiastic – Raffles submits his memo 'On the Administration of the Eastern Islands' – London orders on Singapore still awaited – Raffles seriously ill in Calcutta – returns to Bencoolen

Raffles had been away from Bencoolen for nearly eleven months, the most eventful months in his life. He and Sophia had received but little news of their eldest child, Charlotte, left with Mrs Grimes. She was now eighteen months old and they found her running about. It was Raffles's nature to be very fond of his children, but as we shall see, he lost them, to his great grief. Tropical places like Penang, Bencoolen and Batavia were at that date mortally dangerous for children.

Travers had done wonders with the look of the place. Raffles's predecessor had cut down trees surrounding Government House through fear that bandits might use them as cover in an attack. Now the house stood in a shrubbery of nutmeg, clove, cocoa and cassia. Beyond tall casuarinas, their leaves so like pine needles, sighed in the sea breeze.

But how was Raffles, the protagonist in an imbroglio involving Calcutta and London, going to find scope in so lonely, silent and remote a spot? Would there be more to do than wait for the Court's decision on Singapore? His interests, however, were so varied, his curiosity so wide and his heart so open to the appeal of those whom he had the power to benefit, that he was never at a loss for something to do.

In a letter written at this time to William Wilberforce, whose acquaintance he had made in London, and with whom he had occasionally corresponded since, he discourses on his plans. 'A large proportion of my time has necessarily been devoted to political objects; but in the course of these, neither the cause of the slave nor the improvement of those subjected to our influence, have been forgotten.' He goes on to say that, on first taking up his appointment at Bencoolen, he found it to have been administered no better than the worst Dutch settlements. He began his work of reform by taking the responsibility of emancipating the African slaves imported by the government. Though this was only a beginning, 'the foundation has at least been laid on which a better state of society may be founded.' To help the children of the freed Africans he founded an institution under the Company's chaplain to give them some education. This worked well and had led him to plan schools for the whole population. He has managed, he writes, to win the co-operation of the European residents of Bencoolen, Company's employees, merchants and soldiers, whose prejudice against the native inhabitants, bad at first, was wearing off as they became interested in his projects. He hopes to be able shortly to found a college for upper-class Malays, a college the first of its kind east of India and whose influence, he hopes, will spread throughout the Islands. But these projects of reform will require to be nurtured or indifference will kill them when he is gone. 'I have reason to feel that my health is not likely to carry me through more than five or six years continuance in these Islands.' He asks Wilberforce to take under the wing of his anti-slavery movement this movement of his to liberate the people by education. 'Why should this interesting part of the world be left to slumber in ignorance, while the wilder shores of Africa and the more distant isles of the South Seas invite the attention of the philanthropist?'

Raffles here assumes that British influence will prevail over Dutch in Sumatra. 'Singapore has given us the command of the Archipelago as well in peace as in war; our commerce will extend to every part, and British principles will be known and felt throughout.' Wilberforce stood in his mind for everything that was humane, fair, liberal, just. England was the home of such conceptions, which now that her fleet was invincible and her industrial potential enormously increased by recent inventions, must percolate throughout the world. But without Singapore, he insists, they could not flow east. The Dutch would block the way. They blocked the way no longer.

This letter to Wilberforce reveals Raffles as more than a statesman intent on providing his country with a strong post for extending its commerce. He is a thinker who senses the approach of an Asiatic revolution, greater than the French Revolution, one that will transform all those countries, including the high civilizations of China and Japan, and cause them to imbibe not only what was most useful but, he hopes, the best in western thought and practice. Alone of his contemporaries he has a glimpse of the end of old Asia, its metamorphosis, a commingling of East and West.

Raffles Visits Calcutta

While Raffles's mind was filled with such plans for the future, the news of Bannerman's death came in. Travers reveals in his *Diary* that during Raffles's last visit to Calcutta he and the Marquess of Hastings discussed in its wider aspects the government of the Company's possessions east of India, and that the Marquess agreed that Penang and Bencoolen and, if secured, the station in the Straits, should be placed under one head. As soon as Bannerman retired, he would recommend Raffles for the extended governorship. On receipt, therefore, in October 1819 of the news of his death, Raffles thought it imperative to visit Calcutta.

The letters of this date give us some domestic details. 'Sophia enjoys the best of health and our two children are of course prodigies. Our only anxiety is to take them to England before the climate makes an inroad on their constitutions. Till they are six, seven or eight, they may remain with safety.' In this he was far too sanguine. The letter goes on to say: 'Such portion of my time as is not taken up with public business is principally devoted to natural history. We are making extensive collections in all departments.' Sophia had taken a personal interest and was a great help. He wanted to bring her with him to Calcutta but the ship in port, the only one likely to touch at Bencoolen for many months, was a small brig, with one cabin, the captain's, which he was prepared to share with Raffles. When asked to find room for Sophia he could do no better than offer her a corner of the hold! So Raffles had to set out alone. The voyage was rough and though, as he wrote, he missed her greatly, it was as well she was not with him, 'for it is as much as I can do to stand up against all the privations and annoyances of the vessel'. The voyage lasted from the middle of October till 12 November.

Arrived at Calcutta, Hastings told him that when he had

hinted at giving him Penang, the vacancy was not expected
to occur so soon. The idea of putting all the British settlements east of India under one head had not yet been discussed
with the authorities in London. In the circumstances he had
felt obliged to fill Bannerman's place by appointing a certain
William Phillips, who had been the Colonel's second in command for a long time, and, so, continuing the present system
of separate administrations.

Disappointed over this, Raffles turned his attention to
giving Hastings his views on the situation in the eastern seas.
Though no despatch from the Court on the subject of Singapore had yet reached Calcutta, for the Directors had only
received the news in August, Hastings agreed it would be
prudent to discuss the situation as it might develop after the
recognition of Singapore. He did not doubt it would be
recognized, in spite of Dutch protests through their ambas-
sador in London. Nearly a year had passed since the foundation. It was proving its value month by month. If the Dutch
had ever intended violence, that phase was over. Tempers
had cooled now. There would be a diplomatic wrangle, but
no more. Both in Calcutta and London commercial backing
had grown, supported by the press. The country traders, that
is those in the coast trade as distinct from the main East-West
trade, were the most enthusiastic, for from time to time their
brigs and schooners were fired on by Dutch cruisers when east
of the Straits. Raffles wrote in January 1820: 'With regard to
the commercial men, nothing can exceed the attention I have
received from them; they gave me a public dinner and made
every demonstration to me personally during my stay in
Calcutta.'

He had brought with him a lengthy memorandum entitled
'On the Administration of the Eastern Islands'. The policy he
advocated supposed a free trade, a trade unencumbered by

monopolies and customs dues. If everyone was allowed to trade as he liked, both the inhabitants on land and the merchants coming by sea, commerce would greatly increase. Forced labour, fixed crops and, of course, slavery, were to be out of the question. In such circumstances all the numerous little sultanates from Sumatra to Borneo would leave piracy and turn to exchange of commodities, a vastly more lucrative way of life. Hastings read the memorandum and on 27 November 1819, only a fortnight after Raffles's arrival, repeated his former view that 'the consolidation of our eastern possessions into one government subordinate to the Supreme Authority in India would unquestionably be a desirable arrangement'. As the seat of that government would have to be as far eastward as possible, and so presumably at Singapore, he was precluded from taking any steps until London had communicated to him its decision on the founding of that settlement. He advised Raffles not to spend too much on the place in case it had to be given up and also because the less expense it was, the more favourable would be the view taken by the home authorities. In the end, no doubt, they would agree, as the proposition was so obviously sound. Yet, it was so involved with European politics that an awkward turn there might snuff it out. The peace of 1816 had left the three powerful east European despotisms, Russia, Prussia and Austria, united in what was termed the Northern League. England's security depended on maintaining a balance against their ambitions. Were Holland to fall out with Britain and lean towards the Northern League, England might again be involved in a war on European soil, which she could not afford and would be the ruin of her if it were lost. In Hastings's opinion, however, the situation in Europe was not as delicate as all that and a settlement with the Dutch, leaving Britain with Singapore, could be arranged. But it was necessary to wait; nothing more could be effected at the moment.

As Raffles had done all he could do in Calcutta, he was anxious to get back to Bencoolen. But he fell ill. For some time past he had had severe headaches. Now in Calcutta he had a worse attack than usual. This was brought on by a fit of depression, an unusual experience for him. Where he was staying is not on record, but he evidently felt lonely and missed his family very much. 'I left Lady Raffles and my dear children at Bencoolen three months ago,' he wrote on 17 December 1819 to his friend, the Duchess, 'and I have no one here of congenial feelings with whom I can communicate. I am at this moment heavy and sick at heart.' So depressed was he that he told the Duchess that all he wanted was to return to England as soon as possible and settle down in the country near one of the Duke's mansions. 'I must look out for some cottage or farm and endeavour to sell butter and cheese. Do you think this would do?' It was after writing this that his headaches came on. He was in bed a whole month, the pain in his head being more intense than on previous occasions. The doctors, at a loss to diagnose the cause, fell back on treating him for indigestion. Not till the end of January 1820 was he well enough to embark for Bencoolen.

Chapter Seventeen

DISPLEASURE OF COURT OF DIRECTORS

Raffles's expanding character and views – en route for Bencoolen, stops at the Batta country in Sumatra – writes home about Batta cannibals – his occupations at Bencoolen – happiest period of his life – Court's despatch on foundation of Singapore received in Calcutta February 1820 – Court expresses displeasure but takes no action – Raffles loses his children and becomes very ill – sets out for Singapore – his first pleasure at finding how the town had grown – then discovers Farquhar had not obeyed orders – dismisses Farquhar – John Crawfurd becomes Resident – his character – Departure of Raffles

Carried south on the N.E. monsoon Raffles began to feel much better, though 'as thin as a scarecrow' as he told the Duchess. It was a moment to take stock of his situation. He was not yet forty. How much had happened since he came East fifteen years ago! From deputy secretary he had become a celebrity whose actions were the subject of controversial debate in Penang, Java, Calcutta, London. Whatever he turned his hand to became news. When he pursued his private hobbies, as zoologist, botanist, anthropologist, archaeologist, geologist, explorer or historian, and passed on his observations to London, they aroused deep interest in the learned world. In his official capacity all he touched underwent a transformation. His invariable method was to act in anticipation of sanction. If he received orders he interpreted them to suit his own plans. The result always came as a surprise, though he did not intend to create a sensation. He took what seemed to him the natural course. But as he was an original, his course was unlike other men's. It was not that his aims were unorthodox or unusual. He wanted to see Britain, after victory in Europe, assume her proper station in Asia and apply throughout the East the ideals of free trade and fairness to all, for which she stood or ought to stand. But Britain was not awake to her opportunity and her duties. He had been obliged to stimulate the authorities to accept what seemed to him common sense. He had carried two Governors General with him, first Minto, then Hastings, both of whom had come to admire him, though in Hastings's attitude there remained a trace of misgiving. But he had gone too fast for London to follow. Moreover, his vision kept growing larger. He had begun to visualize vast new fields. Singapore was to be the fulcrum, the pivot of territories to include all Sumatra and Borneo and many sultanates in those waters, an area larger than all India. Its peoples, not stunted as in India by caste, by poverty, by famine, could be lifted from ancient ways, no longer viable, into a new age, born in the West and ready to move eastward. But now, as he rolled south towards Bencoolen, he saw that these extended plans of his were dreams beyond the immediately possible. If he managed to keep Singapore, let the rest wait, let it come in its due time, gradually, slowly. He would be content with Singapore, for Singapore would by itself bring the rest to pass.

But if he had done all that was necessary to do, what now remained for him? To watch over his creation, see that it prospered, wait patiently for London's sanction, hope to be acclaimed at last, perhaps. His intimate friend Travers wrote: 'During this time it was Sir Stamford's intention to remain quiet at Bencoolen.'

His ship had to put in for water at Tapanuli, a very large bay a quarter of the way down the Sumatra coast to Bencoolen. The country here was inhabited by a proto-Malay race called the Battas. His friend Marsden, in his *History of Sumatra*, had said the Battas were cannibals. So had some earlier Portuguese explorers. There was something too in Marco Polo's *Travels* to that effect. Well, here he was on the doorstep of the Batta country. Could cannibalism be prevalent so close? And what was the real meaning of it? Surely more than a mere taste for human flesh? All his anthropological enthusiasm was aroused. He must get to the bottom of the problem. It seems that he had certain agents at Tapanuli whom previously he had instructed to make inquiries. He went ashore, noted down the information the agents had collected and wrote to tell the Duchess and Marsden. To the former he said: 'Before I proceed I must beg you to have a little more patience than you had with Mr Mariner. I recollect that when you came to the story of eating the aunt, you threw the book down. Now I can assure your Grace that I have ten times more to report, and you *must* believe me.' (William Mariner's narrative of his captivity in the Tonga islands in the South Seas had just been published and evidently the Duchess had taken his story of how aunts were eaten for an impudent lie.)

What he goes on to tell her Grace must surely have thrilled her dinner guests at Maiden Bradley. The Battas, he declares, eat their victims alive. They tie them up and bite the flesh off them or cutting a slice here and there dip it in salt and a sauce of lime and chillies and then pop it in the mouth. But,

Raffles assures her, 'the Battas are not a bad people, notwithstanding they eat one another. They are not savages, for they write and read, and think as much or more than those brought up in our National Schools'. Their code of laws makes it obligatory to eat certain criminals and prisoners of war. And he assures her that eating a man alive is not as cruel as some forms of torture until recently attending English executions. But he admits that the Battas' 'state of society is very peculiar', yet is so interesting that later on he plans to go with Sophia deep into their country to make a further study of their customs. 'Should we never be heard of more, you may conclude that we have been eaten.' He is forming a collection of skulls of men who have been eaten. 'Will your Grace allow a few of them room among the curiosities' which he has already sent her? Raffles had a playful side to his character, of which this is an example.

On 11 March 1820 he reached Bencoolen. His wife sums up his situation at this time in the following terms. 'He felt that politically he had done all in his power to promote the best general and national interests of his country in the Eastern Seas; and from this time he devoted himself to the improvement of his little settlement of Bencoolen . . . and indulged in pursuits to which he was always passionately attached. . . . The retirement, the quiet domestic life which he led, soon restored his health; he rose at four in the morning, worked in his garden (in which he always planted all the seeds himself) until breakfast; then wrote and studied till dinner, at which there were always guests. Next, he examined his plantations, accompanied by his children; and often walked about until a late hour of the night.' His children, Charlotte and Leopold, were in the best of health. He wrote: 'Our house is on one side a perfect menagerie, on another a perfect flora; here a pile of stones; there a collection of sea weeds.' At this time he shipped home the whole of his zoological collection, including stuffed tapirs and rhinos, 'as important a consignment as ever sent home'. This went, it seems, to Sir Joseph Banks, the most celebrated naturalist of the day, who entertained the highest opinion of Raffles. 'He is certainly among the best informed of men and possesses a larger stock of useful talent than any other individual of my acquaintance,' he wrote. Raffles, had he lived, would probably have succeeded him as President of the Royal Society. Writing on 18 April 1820 to the Duchess, he has: 'I intend to send you a large consignment (of stuffed animals) by the first favourable conveyance, of which I shall request your Grace's kind care until my return to England.' Describing his menagerie he writes happily of his new orang-outang. 'I have one of the most beautiful little men of the woods that can be conceived; he is not much above two feet high, wears a beautiful surtout of fine white woollen, and in his disposition and habits the kindest and most correct creature imaginable; his face is jet black and his features most expressive . . . always walks erect and would I am sure become a favourite in Park Lane.' The children love him and he hopes to bring him to England.

Though Bencoolen had seemed so depressing at first, he became fond of the place. Sophia in her *Memoir* opines that this period was the happiest in his life. 'He was beloved by all those under his immediate control, who united in showing him every mark of respect and attachment. The natives and Chiefs appreciated the interest he took in their improvement and placed implicit reliance upon his opinions.' As he had no Council, his powers were absolute under the law. But he was very much the benevolent autocrat. Power did him no harm; indeed the more he had, the more he strove to do good. The present health of his family added greatly to his content. A second son was born in May 1820, whom he christened Stamford Marsden but called Marco Polo, and in the following year a daughter he named Ella. 'My children are the finest that ever were seen and if we can manage to take them home in about four or five years we hope to prove that the climate of Bencoolen is not very bad,' he wrote to Marsden on 27 June 1820. His happiness was such that he sometimes had forebodings and warned Sophia it could not last.

The Court's reaction to the founding of Singapore was known in Calcutta in February 1820, a month after Raffles's departure. Hastings was informed that though the Directors were by no means pleased that Raffles had made a settlement on the island of Singapore and considered that he had exceeded his instructions, they were not prepared to annul his action and recall him until further advised by the Governor General.

Hastings saw this despatch as a means of prolonging discussion and putting off action, and continued his wrangle with Capellen, confident that in the long run, with the support of commercial opinion, commonsense would prevail. It was not pleasant for Raffles to hear at this time how Lord Bathhurst, Secretary of the Colonies, had described him in the Lords as a mere trade agent who had caused embarrassment to the government and whom the Dutch should not take seriously. After learning of this he wrote to the Duchess that the feeling of having done his duty compensated him for lack of recognition. He has no ambition but to end his days in peace, engaged on literary and scientific pursuits. If it is his fate to be exposed to the glare of publicity, 'I may become,' he says, 'a greater but not a happier man.' The letter, however, gives the impression he believed that his fame was sure. In a letter dated 17 July 1820 to his cousin, Dr Raffles, he says: 'I learn with much regret the prejudice and malignity by which I am attacked at home for the desperate struggle I have maintained against the Dutch. . . . All however is safe so far. . . . The great blow has been struck . . . the nation must be benefited,' by what he has done. And in another letter: 'After all, it is not impossible that the ministry may be weak enough to abandon Singapore and sacrifice me. I may be recalled, perhaps immediately. But if I cannot carry out my plans here they must prevail in England eventually.'

These citations make it clear that though, as he writes, he 'may personally suffer in the scuffle', he will win in the end. Once the value of Singapore is properly understood, the whole of England will be in its favour. If the controversy drags on a while, so much the better. In two or three years' time Singapore will have become an indispensable British settlement. To give it up now would be idiotic; to give it up then would be a disgraceful humiliation to which the great British public would never submit.

Though the displeasure of the Court was disturbing, it had had no practical results. Nothing more was said about recalling him. Indeed, his position was tolerably strong; he enjoyed the tempered confidence of the Governor General; the commercial communities of Calcutta and, it was now reported, of London were strongly behind him. Though in his letters he may appear to have been somewhat cast down, his wife's estimate of his state of mind was the true one. He was enjoying much happiness. Having her, his children, his hobbies and the pleasure of ruling benignly a trusting people, he had found profound content. But suddenly that happiness was shattered by unexpected events. His three elder children died one after the other. His daughter Charlotte, aged four, died on 13 January 1822; Leopold, aged two years and four

months, died on 5 July 1821; Stamford Marsden, aged a year
and a half, died on 3 January 1822. He was left with his
baby daughter Ella, born early in 1821. Leopold, the first to
die, was carried off in a few hours; which sounds like cholera.
Charlotte died of dysentery after a month's illness. On
15 January 1822 he wrote: 'We have this morning buried our
beloved Charlotte. Poor Marsden was carried to the grave
not ten days before. Within the last six months we have lost
our three eldest children; judge what must be our distress.'
He goes on to say that both he and Sophia have been very ill,
that they must get home as soon as it can be arranged and
that, as the first step, he has sent in his resignation to the Court.
His surviving child, Ella, he is sending home at once. His
plan is to visit Singapore in September 1822, stay there till
June 1823 and, returning to Bencoolen, embark for England
in January 1824, as it will be impossible for the Court's
permission to reach him and his successor to be available
before that.

Raffles became dangerously ill following the shock of his
children's deaths. On 26 February, two days before Ella
sailed for home, he wrote: 'For the last three weeks I have
been confined to my room by a severe fever, which fell on
the brain and drove me almost to madness. I am on my legs
again but am still weak and unable to converse with strangers.'
For some time back he had been afflicted with violent headaches. The present attack was the worst he had experienced.
The day after Ella sailed for England in charge of 'good old
Mrs Grimes', he wrote to the Duchess: 'My heart is sick and
nigh broken.' The rapid stunning sequence of the deaths, the
pains in his head, his wife's desolation, their parting with
their only remaining child, the loneliness and silence of a
remote shore, the fear that they themselves might not reach
England alive – all these together had for the moment

quenched his spirits. But as the year went on he recovered his equanimity.

As planned he set out with Sophia for Singapore on 17 September 1822, travelling via the Straits of Sunda and arriving on 10 October. Three years and three months had elapsed since they had been there, and three years and eight months since the foundation on 6 February 1819. Colonel William Farquhar had remained in charge as Resident. He and Raffles were in regular correspondence, so that the latter had been kept informed how rapidly the settlement was going ahead. As he and Sophia came ashore on 10 October he was delighted with what he saw. 'Here all is life and activity,' he tells the Duchess, contrasting it with Bencoolen where death seemed to reign. 'It would be difficult to name a place on the face of the globe with brighter prospects or more present satisfaction. In little more than three years it has risen from an insignificant fishing village to a large and prosperous town of over 10,000 inhabitants, actively engaged in commercial pursuits.' He tells her of the rising price of land, of the large profits being made, of the numerous ships in port. Later letters give figures. In the first two years and a half 2,839 vessels entered and cleared, 383 owned and commanded by Europeans, the total turnover 8,000,000 dollars. This was spectacular enough, but the figures for the next year (1822) exceeded the total for the two and a half years before, the value of the trade being 8,568,172 dollars, which was greater than for Penang and Malacca put together. The change of air, the excitement of beholding the tremendous success of his foundation, had an exhilarating effect. Both his and Sophia's health improved. His energy recovered, he set to work at once to inspect what Farquhar had done and to give orders for further improvements.

As he went into things, however, he discovered that

Farquhar's administration, though the town itself had advanced rapidly, was not altogether satisfactory. He had left undone matters he had been told to do. He was not thinking on a big enough scale. Moreover, when defects were pointed out to him now, he was disinclined to accept advice from his chief. The success he had achieved had gone to his head. He had begun not only to see himself as the man during whose Residentship Singapore had started to become an emporium for Indian, Siamese and Chinese trade, but to delude himself with the idea that he was the real founder of the place, the originator of the whole conception.

Kind though Raffles was and considerate to his subordinates, he was a man of powerful character. When he found that Farquhar was making difficulties, saying this could not be done, that was impossible, he decided to get rid of him and wrote to Hastings that he should be relieved as he was too small a man to control Singapore, a town of such rapidly growing importance. It had become too much for him; its problems were so different from those he had had to cope with in his former job at Malacca.

Pending orders from Calcutta, Raffles had to put up with him as best he could. But it was not easy in his then state of health. At first the change of air had done him good, but presently his violent headaches began again. The doctors could not diagnose the cause. It may have been some sort of tumour on the brain. In spite of pain and weakness he pressed on with the layout of the streets, the drafting of a constitution, trying so to arrange things before he left that Singapore could expand into the great city he foresaw. Farquhar was like a dead weight. In April 1823 there came a breaking point. Farquhar was in the habit of appearing on official occasions in disreputable old clothes, when he should have worn uniform. This small matter irritated Raffles beyond endurance.

Though he remonstrated with Farquhar, it was no good; he refused to conform. Accordingly Raffles relieved him there and then of his office and himself took over the duties of Resident. Farquhar complained that as he had been appointed by the Governor General, only that authority could remove him. The reply was that Raffles had already sought that authority's sanction. Farquhar gave notice that he would appeal.

Hastings had retired by this date, relieved by Lord Amherst, whom Raffles, it may be recalled, had met while in England at the old Queen's dinner table. By an irony of fate Hastings during his last year was falsely accused of malversation, as had been Raffles by Gillespie in 1813, it being alleged that he was involved in the shady transactions of a banking firm. Though cleared, he resigned, and is said to have left India as heavily in debt as when he came out nine years before. Amherst confirmed the transfer of Farquhar and sent John Crawfurd as Resident. Crawfurd, an East India Company surgeon of scholastic attainments, had served under Raffles in Java and early in 1822 had gone as envoy from the Governor General to the Kings of Siam and Cochin China to negotiate trade agreements. *En route* he had landed at Singapore, where Farquhar repeated to him, as he made a practice of doing to everybody, the fiction that he was the true founder of Singapore. Crawfurd seems to have believed him, for in his book, *Journal of an Embassy to the Courts of Siam and Cochin China*, published six years later, he gives Raffles little or no credit for the foundation. On his way back from Cochin China he called again at Singapore on 16 November 1823 and had talks with Raffles. The mission had been a failure but, as Raffles pointed out, that was of no great consequence, for the trade of Siam and Cochin China was now tapped by Singapore, a free port, to which their merchants were glad to resort, unrestricted by the royal monopolies which strangled commerce inside their own countries.

After a week's stay Crawfurd left for Calcutta, where he got his orders to relieve Farquhar, and he was back in Singapore on 27 May, a fortnight before Raffles left. He had never been one of Raffles's fans. There was rivalry between them in the literary sphere. In 1819 Crawfurd had published in the *Edinburgh Review* a notice on Raffles's *History of Java* in which he pointed out some errors. Raffles had criticized rather severely Crawfurd's *History of the Indian Archaepelago* in the October 1822 issue of the *Quarterly Review*. His private opinion of Crawfurd comes out in a letter to his cousin, Dr Raffles. 'He has considerable talent, an imposing manner, much assurance and assumption. . . . His conclusions are founded on partial views.' It was a fact that Crawfurd was an uncomfortable sort of man, dour in manner and sardonic, with none of Raffles's enthusiasm, warmth and vision. So it was that Raffles found himself handing over his creation to a man not altogether in sympathy with him. However, appearances were kept up during the few days between Crawfurd's arrival and Raffles's departure.

Three days before Raffles left he laid the foundation stone of what was called the Singapore Institution, a Malay College where youths of the Malay upper class would be educated and introduced to western knowledge, and where Europeans could study Malay history, language and art, the plan being to make Singapore a cultural as well as a commercial centre for the Eastern Seas. The necessity of educating the native inhabitants was a new idea and not one that was accepted by those who held it inexpedient to enlighten such people, as it made them discontented with their lot. This short-sighted view was not held by Hastings, who was ahead of his time in his attitude to education, and Raffles, when he discussed the project of the Institute with him in Calcutta in 1819, had his warm support. But London's attitude was unfavourable and Crawfurd, who was not alive to future trends of thought and politics as was Raffles, let the Institute languish for want of support. The foundation ceremony was Raffles's last public act in Singapore. The Sultan and the Temenggong attended. Eighty rupees, collected from those present, were sealed into a hole in the foundation stone and a salute of twelve guns was fired by the battery on the rise where the ancient city had stood.

Abdullah, the youthful Malay clerk who became so attached to Raffles in 1811 at the time of the Java expedition, had moved to Singapore and was now in his direct employ. He was twenty-six years old. When Raffles told him he was shortly leaving Singapore for good, Abdullah was terribly upset. Raffles tried to cheer him up and promised to make sure before leaving that his employment on the staff of the East India Company was made permanent. He now gave him the duty of packing up all his specimens, zoological, botanical, marine, etc., and also his Malay books, of which he had made a large collection, books treating of Malay history, legends, music and drama. In his memoir (the *Hakayit*) Abdullah declares they numbered 309 bound volumes, which filled three trunks six feet in length. In addition were trunks full of Javanese and Bali palm leaf manuscripts, carvings, bronzes, musical instruments and copies of inscriptions. The zoological specimens were numbered in thousands, says Abdullah, who was inclined to exaggerate. Some of the animals were stuffed, some were skeletons. Three trunks contained only stuffed birds. There were several hundred bottles of snakes, scorpions, insects, preserved in spirit. All this packing, Abdullah claims, was done by his own hands. One has to remember, however, that Raffles, throughout his time in

Java and Bencoolen, had sent home many consignments of such objects. What Abdullah packed cannot have been the main collection, but what had been got together during the eight months' stay in Singapore. There were a lot more things in Bencoolen.

Four days before Raffles's departure, Crawfurd presented to him a silver tube containing an address signed by the leaders of the mercantile community, Chinese and European and Malay. It contained the following sentence: 'To your unwearied zeal, your vigilance and your comprehensive views we owe at once the foundation and the maintenance of a Settlement unparalleled for the liberality of the principles on which it has been established.' What three years ago was 'a haunt of pirates has become the abode of enterprise, security and opulence'. The signatories go on to make clear that they fully appreciate what he has done 'in the cause of humanity and civilization', referring in particular to his Institution, and to the measures against slavery which he had taken, where he was ahead of his mother country. 'We cannot take leave of the author of so many benefits without emotion. Accept, Sir, we beseech you, without distinction of tribe or nation, the expression of our sincere respect and esteem.' Addresses presented to departing governors commonly contain encomiums of this sort and, aware of this, the signatories are at pains to declare that so public and outstanding have been Raffles's achievements that 'we cannot be suspected of panegyric'. This may be taken, I think, as a plain statement of fact. Something very extraordinary had happened before their eyes. A city had suddenly come into existence, to which all in that part were flocking, as if to a gold mine, and a gold mine where free shares were guaranteed to all.

Abdullah is the best authority for the final leave-taking

on 9 June 1823. His affectionate warmth pervades a style well fitted to give the emotional atmosphere. The ship was riding in the harbour and Raffles and the onlookers put out to it in boats and sampans. 'Mr Raffles and his Lady embarked, followed by hundreds of people of all races, myself among the rest, as far as the ship; and when they had ascended the ship's side and the crew were raising the anchor Mr Raffles called me to him and I went into his cabin where I observed that his face was flushed, as if he had been wiping his tears. He told me to return and not be distressed: "If it is to be I shall see you again." His Lady now came and gave me twenty-five dollars, saying "I give these to your children in Malacca" and when I heard this my heart burned the more by this act of grace. I thanked her very much, clasping them by the hand in tears and then descended to my sampan and when I had been off some distance I turned round and saw Mr Raffles looking out of the window, when I again saluted him. He raised his hand to me. This was just as the sails were being hoisted; the vessel sailed. Such was my separation from Mr Raffles.' And he goes on to declare that uppermost in his mind was not the sorrow of losing his master but an admiration surpassing all personal feeling for his noble bearing, his justness, modesty and respect for his fellow men. 'There are many great men besides him, clever, rich and handsome, but in good disposition, amiability and gracefulness, Mr Raffles had not his equal, and were I to die and live again such a man I could never meet again, my love of him is so great.'

There does not exist in the vast records of our dealings with eastern peoples so profoundly moving a testimony as this of an Asiatic's love for an Englishman. It is worth a thousand addresses by commercial bodies, a thousand commendations by princes or governments. No decoration ever devised approaches it in value. Raffles never read it, for

Displeasure of Court of Directors

Abdullah's *Hakayit* was written several years later, though what he heard from Abdullah's lips and saw in his streaming eyes told him all.

So Raffles left Singapore never to return, but never to be forgotten. The most astounding aspect of the occasion was that Singapore had not yet been recognized as a British settlement by the Court of Directors and the English government. All this fanfare, these compliments, these emotions about a town which had no legal position, for whose future there was no trace of guarantee, whose inhabitants were there at their own risk, whose founder could not be sure that his devoted labours would not be disowned and himself censured, even ruined – what a paradox! Yet such was the nature of the truly grand departure from Singapore of Sir Stamford Raffles on 9 June 1823. He was forty-two, and had only three more years of life.

Chapter Eighteen

BEREAVEMENTS, DISASTERS
AND RETIREMENT

*En route from Singapore to Bencoolen Raffles calls at
Batavia – the comedy which ensued – Raffles reviews sig-
nificance of Singapore – at Bencoolen birth of fifth child –
Raffles's health continues to decline – applies for permission
to go home to England – death of child – East India Company ship the* Fame *arrives and he embarks for England –*
Fame *goes on fire – Raffles and crew escape in boats to shore
– all his collection lost – leaves two months late on* Mariner
– arrives England

Three days out from Singapore Raffles and his party
were off the coast of Borneo. That route was longer
but safer than through the islands of the Rhio archipelago where they had gone aground last time. Sophia in her
Memoir gives extracts from some of Raffles's letters written
on board. She herself was not too well and was expecting
another child, her fifth. Little Ella was by now safely at home
with her grandparents at Cheltenham. In one of the letters
Raffles mentions that the ship had to put in at Batavia to
discharge cargo. He well knew that the Dutch would not be
pleased to see him; but there was no help for it. The result
was a comic interlude in a drama hitherto wanting in
humorous passages.

Bereavements, Disasters and Retirement

A letter of his dated 28 June, Batavia Road, describes the flutter on shore when his presence was made known to the authorities. 'Had Bonaparte returned to life and anchored in the Downs, it would not have excited greater consternation in England than my arrival has done here'; indeed, he maintains, they were more apprehensive of what he might do than the English would have been of Bonaparte. 'I send you the correspondence which has taken place, as it is rather amusing.'

The first enclosure is his letter to Van der Capellen, the Governor General of Java, announcing that he is in the roadstead as his ship has to deliver a consignment of goods and stating that, as his wife's state of health required a few days on shore, he has sent her to stay with a banker friend of his, Thomas McQuoid. Capellen replied in French: 'J'ai reçu avec une extrême surprise votre lettre. J'étais loin de m'attendre à vous voir arriver à Batavia après tout ce qui a eu lieu depuis 1818. . . . Vous ne pouviez ignorer, Monsieur, qu'une pareille visite ne peut que m'être extrêmement désagréable.' It was quite impossible in all the circumstances for him to consent to a meeting.

Raffles replied at once that he was sorry to have caused His Excellency a disagreeable surprise. He is not asking, however, for an interview and has not the smallest intention of landing. 'There is nothing in your Excellency's conduct which could have rendered me particularly desirous of personal acquaintance.' He is sure, however, that all that Capellen has written against him in despatches was inspired by a wish to serve the interests of his country, and asks that what he has done may be ascribed to the same motives. He hopes that Capellen's dislike does not extend to Lady Raffles and asks that she be allowed to stay on with Mr McQuoid till the ship sails. Capellen, of course, had to agree to this, or appear shockingly ungallant.

The correspondence ended here, but the comedy continued. As soon as the news spread that Raffles was back, crowds of people, English and Dutch, known to him when Lieutenant-Governor of Java, put out to visit him. 'During the week of the vessel's stay at Batavia,' writes Sophia, 'the people of this Island were not to be restrained. Mr Raffles did not once visit the shore, but remained on board and there held as it were a continual levee every day, people of all ranks flocking to him.' Capellen would have liked to prevent this, but was afraid to do so. It was a profound relief to him when the ship weighed and departed on 5 July.

En route for Bencoolen through the Straits of Sunda Raffles committed to paper some reflections upon the immediate past. In one letter he writes of the imbecility and obstinacy of Farquhar and in consequence how dreadfully harassed and fagged he himself became, particularly as his headaches were so frequent. In another letter, however, he declares that what has passed has not altered his regard for Farquhar. 'God knows, I have had but one object in view – the interests of Singapore – and if a brother had been opposed to them, I must have acted as I did towards Colonel Farquhar, for whom I ever had, and still retain, a warm personal affection. I upheld him as long as I could, and many were the sacrifices I made to prevent a rupture, but when it did take place I found it necessary to prosecute my cause with vigour and effect.' Farquhar did not leave Singapore until December 1823, when he went to Calcutta to complain of his supercession and of Raffles having stolen from him the idea of Singapore.

To another correspondent Raffles summarizes what he accomplished at Singapore: 'I had everything to new-mould from first to last,' and he cites his endeavours to insure an honest public service, to settle the various races, each in its own quarter, lay out streets, level ground, drain marshes, see that titles to land were properly registered, draft byelaws and draw up a constitution, in all 'looking a century or two ahead so as to provide for what Singapore may one day become', not only as a great commercial entrepôt, free to all participants in the trade, but 'as the only place in Asia where slavery cannot exist' and as the cultural centre of the Malay race.

Here one perceives the double aspect of Raffles's achievement, political and commercial on the one side, humanistic on the other. The first was concerned to make possible the drive eastwards of British commercial and naval power; the second to bestow upon all who came under her influence the benefits and enlightenment which he conceived that Britain could dispense

The moment was very close when Britain would seek to prise open the door of the closed empire of China. The embassies of Lords Macartney (1793) and Amherst (1816) had failed to improve trading facilities at Canton, the only port where European merchants were allowed to trade, but where the regulations were so restrictive as to be intolerable. The rulers of sovereign states of the Far East wanted to barricade themselves against the inrush of the West, which they perceived would undermine their authority. Singapore provided the means of bringing force to bear, where persuasion was not strong enough. Within twenty years China was to be entered, Hong Kong ceded, a row of treaty ports opened. The West poured into the Far East, effecting an undreamed-of change, the transformation of the whole east by western science, the birth, in fact, of the modern world. Of this Raffles had a glimpse; Singapore was the first, the essential, step towards events of world magnitude. Its foundation was part of a sequence – the Nile, Trafalgar, Waterloo.

Raffles and his party reached Bencoolen on 17 July 1823,

after an absence of nine months. His health was precarious; the intervals between the attacks of pain in his head were shorter. It was essential for him to get home to England as soon as possible if he were to survive. The news from Calcutta was that no ship would be available for six months. He would have to wait probably till January 1824, when an East Indiaman, the *Fame*, would call for him.

In September Sophia's child was born, a daughter, who was christened Flora. Though the delivery was easy, Sophia got a bad fever soon afterwards. On 1 November he wrote: 'We were forced to apply thirty leeches and have recourse to warm baths and laudanum to keep down inflammation,' a treatment very strange to modern ears. 'My health for the last week or two has rather improved, but I am still subject to the same attacks which so often and so completely overpowered me at Singapore.' A fortnight later Sophia was reported still in bed. 'I am scarcely able to hold up my head two days together, but yet we hope that our period of banishment is nearly terminated. If I am fortunate enough to reach England alive, I am certain that no inducement will ever lead me to revisit India.' All he wanted was to get home, hear that Singapore had been sanctioned, and live quietly, perhaps as a farmer. With the accomplishment of his life's work he had no further ambitions. He had done something extraordinary. He was master of an historical event. He needed rest, a long rest. Dating from 1795, when at fourteen he had entered the East India House, he had thirty years' service.

To fill the time of waiting for the *Fame*, he began to write a full account of how he founded Singapore. Though he had heard no more about the Court's final view, he took hope, for he felt he could rely upon the powerful aid of the London mercantile houses. Bencoolen was an extremely unhealthy place and his letter refers to the deaths of several of his staff. These losses he felt severely but, he writes on 10 December, 'the worst of all has been the loss of our only remaining child in this country. The shock has been too much for us. We are both so ill ourselves that neither of us dares quit the room. Our spirits are completely broken and we are most anxious to get away from such a charnel house. Either I must go to England, or by remaining die.' Detained beside the graves of four of his children on that remote and lonely shore, a claustrophobic terror overwhelmed him for the moment. Afterwards his wife wrote: 'It is not easy to describe the anxiety in which the last two months were spent . . . seeing hour after hour pass away, without the means of escape, and with scarcely a hope that life would be prolonged from one day to another.' Such was an out-station in those days. No matter how ill you were, there was nowhere to go to; you could not get out of it.

Early in January 1824 a vessel, the *Borneo*, came into port to load pepper for England. She was inconvenient and small, but afraid they would be dead before the *Fame* arrived, if she ever did, Raffles decided to charter her and be off. When about to ship his luggage and the large number of cases containing his collection, now much augmented by the cases stored at Bencoolen, the *Fame* appeared. This was an immense relief. The *Fame* was in comparison a roomy ship and altogether more suitable for the long voyage via the Cape of Good Hope. As it turned out the *Borneo* made a safe landfall in England. A few days more and they would have sailed in her. *Dis aliter visum.*

At daybreak on 2 February 1824 they set out for home on the *Fame*, all the hundreds of cases stowed and a number of animals in cages, including a tapir, an animal new to England. The crew numbered about forty. There was a cargo of saltpetre in the hold. By nightfall they had covered fifty miles on a north-westerly course. Sophia was already in bed and Raffles was undressing when, at 8.20 p.m., there was a cry of fire, fire! Raffles rushed out and saw flames coming from the hold below the cabins. They were already beyond control. The Captain immediately ordered the boats to be lowered. The long boat, much the most capacious of the three on board, was too near the fire to swing out, but the two others were shortly in the water. There was not time to take anything. Sophia, in her nightdress, was lowered into one of the boats; Raffles followed, half dressed as he was. The boat filled with some twenty others. 'All this passed much quicker than I can write it,' says Raffles in his account of the disaster. 'We pushed off and as we did so, the flames burst out of our cabin window. The whole of the after part of the ship was in flames. The masts and sails were now taking fire.' The captain and the rest of the crew were seen getting into the other boat. 'We hailed her,' writes Raffles, 'have you all on board? "Yes, all save one." 'A seaman was below sick in his cot. There seemed no possibility of saving him. 'At this moment the poor fellow, scorched by the flames, roared out most lustily, having run upon deck.' He jumped and was picked up by the captain's boat.

So here were the two boats, much overloaded by the forty persons in them, with night fallen and fifty miles from shore. The captain, however, had a compass, he knew his position and set a course. The seamen settled down to an all-night row. There was no water or food in the boats. Unless they could make Bencoolen by the next day they were exposed to many dangers. The sea was fairly calm, but the wind might freshen at any moment. There were rapid tides down the coast of Sumatra which might sweep them south of Bencoolen where for a long distance the coast was rocky.

Bereavements, Disasters and Retirement

As they looked back the ship, now a mass of flames, lit
up the sky. The magazine exploded but she still floated.
When the saltpetre caught fire the blaze 'illuminated the
horizon in every direction, casting a blue light over us. The
men behaved manfully. They rowed incessantly, and with
good heart, and never did poor mortals look out more for
daylight and for land than we did.'

With dawn they saw the coast, though they were a distance
south of Bencoolen. However, at nine o'clock a vessel put
out to rescue them. Aboard it, they soon made the shore,
where a sympathetic crowd awaited them. 'There was not
a dry eye,' says Raffles, immensely touched and taking the
warm welcome as a proof that his administration of Bencoolen had been well liked. They were in bed by three and
did not wake till six the next morning.

Raffles had no difficulty in counting his losses. He had lost
everything. All his official papers and valuables, such as the
ring given him by the Princess Charlotte, were gone; notes
for a history of Sumatra and Borneo; his account of the
founding of Singapore; grammars, dictionaries, maps, his
natural history specimens with 2,000 drawings. 'There was
scarce an unknown animal, bird or fish or plant, which we
had not on board; a living tapir, a new species of tiger,
splendid pheasants. All, all has perished.' The labour, the
scholarship, research of years, destroyed in a single night!
Nothing had been insured, as this had not been possible at
Bencoolen.

The only thing to be done was to find another ship as
soon as possible, and once at home to appeal to the gener-
osity of the Company. Not till April, more than two months
later, did a ship become available. During the interval Raffles
was not idle. 'Misfortune,' wrote Sophia, 'seemed to have
no other effect on Sir Stamford than to rouse him to greater

exertion.' The very next morning after the disaster he began a fresh map of Sumatra, set his draughtsmen to work making new natural history drawings and sent men into the forest to collect more animals.

On 10 April 1824 Raffles and his party left Bencoolen for England at last on board the *Mariner*. Just before he sailed he was cheered by a letter from Lord Amherst, the new Governor General, commending him for his services and expressing regret at his departure. Farquhar, having failed to persuade Amherst to interfere on his behalf, left Calcutta the same week to seek redress in London.

Raffles's health, bad for a long time, had further deteriorated under the stresses of calamity. But, writes Sophia, the energy of his mind was not reduced. After twelve days of rest and sea air he recommenced his studies with vigour. Incredible as it may seem, he worked for two hours before breakfast at 9 a.m. on Euclid and logic, followed by Greek, Latin or Hebrew. From 10 a.m. to 11 a.m. he made notes on those studies, and from 11 a.m. to 1 p.m. he was engaged in writing an account of his administration in Java and Bencoolen. After an hour's lunch interval he read on general subjects till 4 p.m. when he had dinner and walked the deck for exercise till 7 p.m. In the cool of the evening he would read out something entertaining to Sophia and be in bed by 10 p.m.

This rigorous programme, a sort of refresher course in the humanities, he had to abandon in the region of the Cape. The *Mariner* ran into an appalling gale lasting three weeks, so violent that Sophia had to have the side of her bunk boarded up and ropes provided to hang on to, and so terrifying that 'we resigned ourselves to the feeling that our pilgrimage in this world was soon to close'. They put into Cape Town where they stayed a week to recuperate and reached St Helena on 25 June 1824, two and a half months out from Bencoolen.

Bereavements, Disasters and Retirement

The island had reverted to anonymity; Napoleon had died in 1821. After a week's stay they continued the voyage and reached Plymouth on 20 August 1824. 'Here we are, thank God, safe and sound,' he wrote to a friend, 'and in better health than could have been expected.' He was suffering at the moment only from writer's cramp, but his headaches, in fact, were no better. He wrote the truth to the Duchess on 24 August. 'My constitution is terribly shattered. Nevertheless, I live in confidence that as the spirit is good, the body will yet mend. How happy shall I be to see you once more.' They hurried by post-chaise to Cheltenham, where Sophia's parents were waiting for her, and found their little girl, Ella, the only survivor of the family of five, 'all that our fondest wishes could have desired'.

Chapter Nineteen

DEATH OF RAFFLES IN LONDON

The big news was that on 17 March 1824 a final settlement had been reached with the Dutch on the subject of Singapore, after discussions covering four years. It was effected by an exchange of possessions. The Dutch sphere of influence was to be south of the equator. The island archipelagos, including Sumatra south of that line and so including Bencoolen, were declared to be Dutch. Malacca, which in 1816 had been returned to Holland, was now transferred back to Britain, and her right to keep Singapore was acknowledged. Some further minor adjustments were made, including the cession to Britain of certain small Dutch settlements on the coast of India. The gate to China was secured for England.

Death of Raffles in London

The treaty was not everything that Raffles had dreamed of, but the main point was gained. His creation, Singapore, and all that it signified, was safe. He wrote to Canning, the Foreign Secretary, that he agreed the treaty was just in its principles and satisfactory in its terms. Canning replied that he was very gratified to learn that such was Raffles's view. 'There could be no more competent judgment than yours.' And he went on to declare that 'your extreme activity in stirring difficult questions and the freedom with which you committed your Government without their knowledge or authority to measures which might have brought a war upon them unprepared, did at one time oblige me to speak my mind to you in instructions of no very mild reprehension,' but that was long forgotten and he now commended 'his zeal and ability'. In other words, Raffles had taken a gamble, which at the time made the Government feel nervous, but since it succeeded all was well. Coming from a Foreign Secretary this amounted to a handsome *amende honorable*. As we know, Raffles's foundation of Singapore was not, in fact, so dangerous a move as to lead to a war between Holland and England. The Dutch were outwitted and forestalled, and consequently annoyed. But they believed that diplomacy would suffice to put all right, for their information was that Raffles's action would be disowned. War was never seriously contemplated by any responsible Dutch statesman. That the British Government thought there was such a risk or that the *entente* with Holland would be damaged, was a misapprehension. Moreover, the importance of Singapore was not realized at first nor the necessity of acting quickly if it was to be secured. Since an immediate occupation of the island was essential, and to obtain London's sanction would have taken more than a year, what else could Raffles have done but act on his own responsibility? Men of superior talent

and force of character always act so. That is how history is
made.

Honourable though Canning's *amende* might be, nothing
was said of rewarding Raffles. His services were now recognized as pre-eminent, though the full value of Singapore as
providing the British navy with the means of attaining
supremacy in eastern seas, and all that meant – the curbing of
piracy and the oriental trade in slaves, and the support of
British commerce in its search for wider markets in China –
had still to be fully demonstrated. But if in 1817 on his return
from Java there was talk of his being raised to the peerage,
surely now after the acknowledgement of his services by the
Foreign Secretary, representing both Parliament and the
Board of Control, it would have been natural to make him a
baron? The Court of Directors had not yet spoken. Perhaps
after they had done so, had handsomely rewarded him and
also compensated him for his losses while on their service, the
Ministry would see it as the moment to recommend him to
the King for a title. The King was his old patron, who as
Regent had knighted him in 1817. He would be happy that
his protégé had done so well and would agree at once to
confer the honour, if he did not himself suggest it. Had not
Raffles been one of the best friends of his lamented daughter,
Charlotte, whose extraordinary tomb in St. George's Chapel,
Windsor, testifies today to his grief at her loss? She wanted to
make Raffles a lord. Here was his opportunity to carry out
the wish of his dead daughter, his only child.

But what happened was very different.

After a stay of a month in Cheltenham, Raffles and Sophia
felt well enough to go on a short visit to London. It was
essential to call without delay on the Directors of the Court
of the East India Company. Getting no final answer out of
them all these years had become a nightmare. An interview

with the Chairman, William Astell, was arranged. In the past he had taken Raffles's part and some half dozen other Directors were known to be friendly. Raffles hoped for full recognition of his services to the Company, which so far he had never received, and some compensation for his losses on the *Fame*, if possible in the form of a pension.

After a talk with Astell he wrote: 'The feeling, I am glad to say, seems very general in my favour. The Directors are a large heavy body and move slowly. I must not complain of their delay.' He was aware that prejudice against him lingered in certain quarters, or at least a reluctance to admit that the Court had been wrong in advising against Singapore, but he thought it hard to have to suffer for their lack of vision, though, he wrote, 'I shall not be the first public servant to be neglected by the higher powers.' He left the East India House resigned to await their decision with patience. Those friendly to him on the Court had assured him of their support. Everybody in the building was not a narrow old merchant. Charles Lamb, now a famous literary figure, was still a clerk there. (He retired the following year on a pension of £450 per annum.)

Back in Cheltenham he had another bad attack of pains in the head which confined him to bed for several weeks. There was no sign that the return to his native air was curing him. If, as is believed, he was suffering from some sort of tumour on the brain, the English climate and the waters of Cheltenham could be no cure. Nor could the surgery of that date afford relief, supposing a correct diagnosis were made. His former secretary, Travers, now resident in Ireland as his wife was Irish, came over to see him. After the visit he noted in his diary: 'I left very fearful that my valued friend's constitution was too much undermined to ever get properly re-established. He seemed a complete skeleton.' However,

Farquhar's Appeal

Raffles was strong enough to complete a long memorandum, *Statement of Services*, as an *aide-mémoire* for the Court.

In November, as Cheltenham was too much out of the way, he moved to London and rented a furnished house in Piccadilly. For the moment he was feeling better. But now he had some bother with Farquhar, who had arrived in London to petition the Court. He had become a trying old person with a grievance, rather muddled and very obstinate. A copy of his petition was presently forwarded by the Court to Raffles for comment. It began by complaining of the 'flagrant injustice and tyranny' he had suffered at the hands of Raffles and asserting his own forbearance on all occasions, even when he was demonstrably in the right. He repeated the fable that it was he who had suggested the founding of Singapore and who, as Resident, had nursed it into its present prosperity. In 1822 when Raffles came from Bencoolen to inspect his work at Singapore, 'he commenced a course of conduct which, to an officer of your Memorialist's rank and experience in the affairs of the Company could not fail to be in the highest degree offensive.' As a final injustice, Raffles reported him to Calcutta for incompetence and suspended him. He pleads that only by posting him back to Singapore can justice be done.

Raffles's reply was long and detailed. He felt that Farquhar's charges, even if not exactly believed, might create an unfavourable impression, coming as they did at the very moment when his own case was before the Court. The best answer, he said, to the claim that Farquhar had 'suggested, nurtured and matured' the foundation of Singapore was that there was not a single word in the mass of official papers on the subject to support such a claim. They provided a detailed, precise, almost day-to-day account of exactly how Singapore was founded. 'I entreat your Honourable Court will do me the justice to peruse the correspondence between Colonel Farquhar and myself.' It will prove, moreover, that he was given every opportunity of explaining and justifying his administration. 'It became my unpleasant duty to undo almost everything he had done.'

On being sent a copy of Raffles's statement, Farquhar made a brief rejoinder, after which the Court dismissed his appeal. He had to content himself with a routine rise in his military rank. The plain fact was that he had never occupied a position in which he could have planned and undertaken the foundation of Singapore and that when he was given charge of it as Resident, subject to Raffles's supervision and orders, he was unable to rise to so novel an occasion because he had not the mind of a statesman. He thought it enough to administer the young dynamic settlement in the same easygoing, dilatory, haphazard way he had administered for fifteen years old half-dead Malacca. With an obstinacy characteristic of elderly men of his type, he renewed in 1830, after Raffles's death, his claim to be the true founder of Singapore in an article in the *Asiatic Journal*, which at his request was republished in the *Singapore Chronicle*, whose editor, however, pointed out its fatuity. He died in 1839, aged sixty-eight.

While the Farquhar case (almost as trying as the Gillespie case) was going on, Raffles moved from the rented house in Piccadilly to 23 Lower Grosvenor Street, whose thirty-year lease he bought. Between his relapses he felt wonderfully energetic. He even thought of standing for Parliament. The Duchess advised him to take it easy. 'Be idle,' she wrote, 'and go out a great deal when it is fine. Pray do not unpack too much.' He had told her that he had 171 cases of specimens still to unpack. If these were what he had collected in Bencoolen between the burning of the *Fame* and his departure by the *Mariner* two months later, he had replenished his losses more than might have been expected.

The year 1824 passed into 1825. The Court remained silent on his memorial; he, whenever not in pain, took an active interest in people and causes. He made friends with Dr Morrison, the sinologue, first to teach the Chinese language in England. He also set to work on founding a London zoo. His old friend, the great naturalist and President of the Royal Society, Sir Joseph Banks, had died in 1822 and his place had been taken by Sir Humphry Davy. He and Raffles collaborated to launch the zoo, which was not to be just a menagerie but a Society for the study of Zoology. Davy took charge of the practical side of the business, Raffles the scientific. He wanted an institution better than the Jardin des Plantes, the Parisian zoo, which he had visited in 1817. Before leaving for Sumatra he had often discussed the subject with Banks. Moreover, he had sent home animals from Sumatra to be kept until such a zoo was opened. He wrote in the prospectus now: 'We have as yet attempted little and effected almost nothing on behalf of the student of zoology or the philosopher', despite the many British settlements in the East and many ships coming and going. A piece of land near the metropolis, to be called the Zoological Gardens, was acquired. Subscriptions were raised and the project was realized soon afterwards. Raffles was elected the first President; his bust today is in the Lion House.

At the time of his 1817 stay in London Raffles became, as we have seen, a figure in society. His subsequent achievements made him yet more of a celebrity and his escape from the burning *Fame*, which had been reported at length in the English press, added a sensational interest. Everybody had heard that dramatic story and how he had lost all his personal possessions. So, on moving into 23 Lower Grosvenor Street, he received invitations of all kinds. In April–May 1825 hardly a day passed without a dinner appointment. He loved parties and meeting people, but such a round of gaiety was soon too much for him. The sooner he got out of London to the quiet of the country, the better. He had already decided to buy a house and property of 112 acres called High Wood at Hendon, then a rural village, at a cost of some twenty thousand pounds. He moved there on 25 July 1825 but did not give up the house in Lower Grosvenor Street. 'Prudence dictates the necessity of keeping as quiet as I can. A few months in the country may set me up again,' he wrote. His attention had been drawn to High Wood by William Wilberforce, who had purchased an adjoining property. They would be next door neighbours and divide Highwood hill between them. There was no one he would rather have as his neighbour, he said. In 1811 Wilberforce had succeeded in getting trade in slaves made a criminal offence. The slaves already on the plantations, however, were not freed, and it was for their emancipation that he was now striving.

Raffles's first guests at High Wood were Thomas McQuoid and his family, who had just arrived from Java. McQuoid had been banking £16,000 of Raffles's money, which he was asked to transfer to London through his banking associates in Calcutta. 'The best way to get to my house,' Raffles wrote to him, 'is to take a chaise up the Edgeware Road from Tyburn Turnpike and on reaching the centre of Edgeware village, some eight miles out of town, turn right and in 3 miles you are at Highwood House.' It was a pleasant country drive. At that date London had less than a million inhabitants.

Raffles had started farming as soon as he moved in July. The estate, as he bought it, was a going concern, fully stocked and planted, with its supply of barns, implements and labour. 'The change of air, sun and interest have already worked an amendment in my health,' he writes on 15 August 1825. Sophia looks after the poultry and pigs, he sees to the crops. 'We brew our own beer and bake our own bread and lead an entire country life.' The farm, he calculated, ought to yield him a net profit of over £600 a year. What the East India Company might add remained uncertain. He hoped for a pension of at least £500 a year, but could not count on getting it, even though £500 was only half what a senior officer of the Company in Bengal received after twenty-two years' service. He had been in the east from April 1805 till April 1824, nineteen years, with leave in the middle from March 1816 till March 1818. It appears that under the regulations he could not claim a pension by right. In his memorial he asked for it as compensation for losses. William Astell, who favoured the grant, had unfortunately retired that very year from the chairmanship of the Court. Raffles had written to Thomas Murdoch, a friend on the directorate, to use his influence with the new chairman, Sir George Robinson. Other powerful friends he also canvassed, writing, for instance, to the Marquess of Hastings, now, as recorded, Governor of Malta. Hastings excused himself, declaring that he had little influence, as he was on 'strange terms' with the Court after the unpleasant events which had led to his resignation of the Governor-Generalship. Charles Wynn, an ex-President of the Board of Control, was also addressed and his reply was that the Board, though it had power to cut down grants, had none to inaugurate or increase them. George Canning, the Foreign Secretary, promised to speak to Sir George Robinson, but feared he would pay little attention in a matter which exclusively concerned his own department.

These replies left Raffles apprehensive that prejudice against him remained strong behind the scenes. He had offended the Court by going his own way. He had had to go his own way or nothing would have been done. Now he was asking a favour of people little disposed to admit they had been wrong. He knew all this well enough and could only await the issue, living as quietly as his active mind permitted.

Wilberforce did not move into his Highwood hill property until 1826 but they saw a good deal of each other as Raffles helped him to lay out his estate. The village at the top of the hill was divided between them, Wilberforce having the Crown·public house and Raffles The Rising Sun. Both estates fell within the parish of Hendon, the vicar of which had his money in the slave plantations of the West Indies, and for that reason was on far from cordial terms with the famous advocate of emancipation, which, if it became law (as it did in 1833), would deplete his income. Raffles, as Wilberforce's friend and supporter, was also a target for his animosity.

Early in the New Year (1826) Raffles felt he must get back to London for a bit. In a letter of 7 February he wrote that he was feeling better than at any time since his return from the East and that he intended to move into town next day for the London season, staying till the end of May, if his health allowed. There was still no news about a pension from the East India House. But in March came news of an opposite sort. The merchant-banker business in Batavia belonging to his friend McQuoid was reported bankrupt. The smash occurred before the firm had remitted the £16,000 standing to Raffles's credit, and which represented a large part of his remaining capital. Travers, who had some money also in the McQuoid business, was summoned from Ireland early in April to attend a meeting of the creditors in London. He called on Raffles as soon as he arrived. 'One striking difference,' he wrote, 'in my friend Sir Stamford was that although his spirit and animation were great, his articulation was at times heavy and thick.'

McQuoid was present at the creditors' meeting, looking very miserable at having failed the man he was so fond of. 'The affairs of the house appear to have been but indifferently managed,' was Travers's view and he added with an asperity unusual for him: 'I fear my friend McQuoid is but ill calculated for a merchant.' It became evident that Raffles would never see even a penny in the pound of his £16,000.

Only a day or so afterwards, 12 April 1826, two letters arrived from the Court. The first dealt with Raffles's services to the Company. It will be recalled that some time back the Court, while concurring with the Indian government that nothing could be said against his public character, had deferred expressing an opinion on the merits of his administration. The present letter was devoted to this latter subject and under the three heads of Java, Sumatra and Bencoolen gave the Court's opinion, which amounted to an approval of a curiously qualified kind. The letter began by declaring that the success of Minto's expedition against Java in 1811 was promoted by the information supplied by Raffles and advanced by the plans he drew up. His measures to overcome financial difficulties in the new conquest were sound, with the possible exception of the sale of lands. His reform of the judicial system was praiseworthy. In Sumatra his internal reforms were approved. But his political measures were another matter. Of them the Court had already expressed disapprobation, though it must admit that he was actuated by a zealous solicitude for British interests in the Eastern Seas. Such was also his motive in founding Singapore, a political venture which had turned out well, though it might not have. That it did, was 'a strong point in his favour' which the Company was willing to put on record despite the fact of its initial disapproval.

The wording of the Court's letter is here very vague, but

it seems to mean that though the Company could not condone the way Raffles had acted without its previous sanction, the success of Singapore went a certain distance to palliate his behaviour.

The letter's attitude to his anti-slavery measures has the same devious twist. He is censured for having emancipated the Company's slaves in Sumatra, for he was not authorized to do so, yet his zeal for the abolition of slavery must be approved. No criticism attached to his exertions in the interests of literature and science, which were 'highly honourable to him'.

In this judgment the Court viewed Raffles as it might have any humdrum official for whom a tepid approbation, interspersed with reproofs, was proper and sufficient. No doubt he was a well-meaning fellow; his humanitarian principles did him credit. But he had wilfully ignored the East India Company and could not expect to be rewarded by it. He asked for a pension in compensation for his losses. His losses were due to mischance. It could only ignore such an extravagant claim.

The second letter, which came the same day as the first, was like a communication from an Accountant General. Far from the Company owing Raffles any money for services, compensation or the like, he owed the Company a substantial sum. The letter was a demand that he now pay it. The reader will find it tedious to be asked at this stage of a narrative, moving rapidly to its close, to pause and examine the letter in detail. Yet the main points must be given, if what followed is to be fully intelligible. The Governor General had allowed Raffles to draw salary totalling some six thousand pounds for the two years (1816–18) when he was on leave in England between his appointments of Lieutenant-Governor of Java and of Lieutenant-Governor in Bencoolen. There were pre-

cedents in support of disbursements to officers on leave and
Raffles thought it probable that the Governor General's
recommendation that he draw the money would be endorsed
in London. Nevertheless, in case it should not be, he had
deposited government securities with the Accountant General
of Bengal to cover the sum. The Court now over-ruled the
Governor General and demanded repayment with interest.
No reason was given why the demand had not been presented
long ago nor why interest was charged, although the delay
in repayment was not Raffles's fault but due to the dilatoriness
of the Court in demanding it. However, as Raffles had set
aside money in case he would have to pay, the demand was
not as great a hardship as it might have been. But there were
other items, which brought the total to be repaid to about
£22,000. The Governor General had allowed Raffles to draw
£3,313 to cover depreciation in the medium of exchange
used to pay his salary in Java. This was now disallowed by
the Court. In Bencoolen he had been permitted by the same
authority to draw £6,914 as a commission on exports and
£4,670 for expenses, chiefly incurred in founding Singapore.
These figures added with the rest gave the twenty-two
thousand total. Raffles had made no provision here and so had
to find about fifteen thousand. As he had just lost sixteen
thousand through McQuoid's bankruptcy, this demand was
not easy to meet. Had the Court been only a little more
prompt in presenting their bill he could have drawn out the
money before McQuoid failed. In his reply, dated 29 April,
he informed the Court that he would immediately direct his
agents to realize the securities deposited with the Accountant
General and pay the £6,000, plus interest. For the £15,000
residue he would sell what shares he had in India stock and
also 'the little property I had set apart as provision for my
family after my death'. Here he seems to have been thinking

of his town house rather than of High Wood. He followed his letter of 29 April with another dated 16 May in which he gave more detailed reasons why, in particular, the disallowance of expenses for the founding of Singapore was unfair. For him to have to pay out of his own pocket for what had already proved so valuable for the China trade could surely not be the intention of the Honourable Company.

But it was the intention and the Court did not abate its demands. Raffles was called upon to meet the total bill.

It has been the rule among writers of Raffles's life to declare that the shock of these demands killed him, for he died three months after receiving the Court's letter of 12 April 1826. It is difficult, however, to reconcile this theory with the facts. In the first place, Raffles was a dying man when he received the demand for £22,000. The tumour on his brain was bound to kill him soon, shock or no shock. For at least six years, ever since the bad attack he had in Calcutta in January 1820, it had been slowly but surely growing worse. The symptoms remained the same—violent pain in the head, so violent as to keep him in bed for weeks, followed by periods, sometimes of two or three months, with little or no pain, when he was immensely active and also very high spirited, happy, optimistic and confident. Even when the deaths of four of his children were added to his physical sufferings, he resisted melancholy and never surrendered to despair. Not the worst pain, not the worst grief, could crush him. His was too resilient a character to succumb to the shock of receiving a demand for twenty-two thousand. He had survived many worse shocks. Moreover, as one has seen, he had money, put aside purposely, to meet a quarter of the demand, and enough in stock and estate to cover the rest without touching his house and farm on Highwood hill, a property sufficient to maintain him. Moreover, he had a host of friends and admirers, and a solid reputation in many fields, which would ensure the offer of further appointments if he managed to remain alive. That he was able to make light of his situation is seen in a letter to his cousin, Dr Raffles, dated 15 June 1826, two months after receiving the Court's demand: 'I have had a great deal to annoy me since I saw you last; but it is a worldly affair and I trust will not affect our happiness.' When he died three weeks later, it was not from shock, which his temperament had enabled him already to surmount, but from the mortal distemper which he had borne so lcng with fortitude and with a dignity which was profoundly moving.

Evidence of dates also shows conclusively that the demand of 12 April 1826 had little effect on his nerves. He stayed on in London and much enjoyed the season. On 18 May he wrote to Dr Raffles: 'Seldom a day passes without an engagement for dinner. . . . All is so new, varied and important in the metropolis of this great empire, after so long a sojourn in the woods and wilds of the East that, like the bee, I wander from flower to flower.' Of these last months of his life Sophia writes: 'His sense of enjoyment was as keen as ever, his spirit as gay, his heart as warm, his imagination still brighter, though his hopes in this world were less.' He knew he was dying but no fear of death could depress him. How then suppose it true that a dunning letter from a group of men who had always obstructed him and whom he had always circumvented, could knock him out? It is as unlikely to be true as the myth that in 1823, three years before, an adverse criticism of his poems in the *Edinburgh Review* killed John Keats, already doomed to an early death by the state of his lungs. Sophia, in her lengthy, well documented and thorough *Memoir* of her husband, does not mention the demand for twenty-two thousand or even hint that any transaction between him and the Court had an appreciable effect on his health. What may have given rise to the view that the Court's harsh letters were responsible for his death was the fact that about 20 May he fainted when on his way home from one of his cheerful parties and was brought unconscious to his house in Lower Grosvenor Street. He remained unconscious for an hour but came to after being bled. It was an apoplectic fit or slight stroke, Sophia records, the cause of which was the tumour and the fact of his being overtired. As he wrote a few days later to his cousin, the attack reminded him that he had been 'quite long enough in London with its dissipations and excitements. A few months in the country and on the farm will set me up again'. They were back at High Wood shortly afterwards. The view that this preliminary stroke was due to shock over the Court's demand is thus seen to have no support. It happened 'when his heart was full of enjoyment', as Sophia puts it.

A month after their return to High Wood Raffles had a second and fatal stroke. The account of what happened is to be found in Travers's diary and in a sort of obituary in the *Gentleman's Magazine* for July 1826. On 4 July he went to bed as usual between 10 and 11 p.m. There was nothing in his appearance or manner to suggest the imminence of a fatal attack. At five o'clock next morning Sophia was told that he was not in his room. She got up at once to investigate and found him lying dead at the bottom of the stairs. It was the day before his forty-fifth birthday.

On the evidence of an autopsy, carried out by a leading specialist of the day, it was declared that death was caused by an apoplectic stroke brought on by an abscess on the brain.

Chapter Twenty

SHABBY BEHAVIOUR OF
EAST INDIA CO.

*Funeral of Raffles in Hendon church – The refusal of the
vicar to allow a memorial tablet – whereabouts of Raffles's
coffin forgotten – its rediscovery in 1914 – statue in Westminster Abbey – Sophia asked to pay Court's bill of 12 April
– her offer of ten thousand pounds accepted – The extreme
meanness of the Court's action – Sophia's* Memoir *– her
death*

As Raffles was resident in the parish of Hendon,
he was buried in Hendon church. The vicar, the
Rev. Theodore Williams, whose private income, as
has been said, came from a slave plantation and in consequence who was on chilly terms with Raffles, did not conduct
the burial service himself, but asked a certain Rev. J. Roseden
to officiate. There is no evidence that Raffles's death caused
any stir outside the circle of his family and friends. As
Travers noted in his *Diary*: 'He was not generally known.'
Though a man of genius, whose place in history was assured,
he was not a public figure in England, like a Prime Minister
or a victorious General. He had not even the local popularity
of a preacher with an enthusiastic congregation, like his
cousin Dr Raffles, whose funeral in 1863 was attended by
fifty thousand persons. Even well-informed people had but a

vague idea of what had happened at Singapore. The desert island's rise had only begun; it had already more trade than Penang and Malacca combined, but its phenomenal growth into one of the ten largest cities in Asia, when it left Calcutta far behind, was in the future. Raffles's reputation as an administrator and a humanitarian had been made six thousand miles away; his standing as a natural scientist was only with a select few. For all such reasons the funeral, which took place on 12 July 1826, was very quiet. It had none of the show belonging to the sepulture of a nation's great man, was as unnoticed as Keats's funeral in 1821 or Shelley's in 1822. The Rev. Roseden did his part, read the burial service, its splendid passages of immortal prose comforting the weeping Sophia and her daughter and the little gathering of relations and close friends more than would have the presence of a large fashionable congregation. The lead coffin, encased in wood, to which was attached a brass plate with Raffles's name and the date of his death, was not buried in the earth of the churchyard but placed in a vault which the family had purchased. Application was made to the Rev. Theodore Williams for permission to erect a memorial tablet inside the church to mark the position of the tomb below. He had been obliged to allow the burial, as Raffles was a parishioner, but the tablet was within his discretion to refuse. He did refuse. He would not tolerate in his church a tablet to a man so unfeeling as to advocate, to the cruel detriment of those who had invested their savings in a Negro plantation, the emancipation of its slaves. The reverend gentleman should have considered more carefully his own posthumous reputation and not have risked the eternal obloquy which is now his. This malicious fellow continued as vicar of Hendon for another fifty years, dying in 1876 at the age of ninety-one, a hoary relic of the age of slavery. During those fifty years he maintained his refusal to sanction a tablet. By the end of them Sophia was dead and the position of the vault forgotten. Not till 1914, when the church was being enlarged, was the vault opened and Raffles's coffin discovered. The outside wooden coffin had decayed, leaving the nameplate lying loose on the inner lead coffin. Application was then made for permission to carve on the stone floor immediately above the vault the inscription to be seen there today which shortly describes Raffles as founder of Singapore.

But while anonymity reigned at Hendon, admirers of Raffles in 1832 commissioned Mr Chantrey (afterwards Sir Francis Chantrey) to carve a marble statue of him seated in a chair, with a laudatory inscription underneath. This was placed in Westminster Abbey in the north aisle within the iron gates behind the choir screen, where it now is. Though a work of only moderate artistic merit, the statue is important as showing that within eight years of his death Raffles was considered worthy of a place in the Abbey. The inscription, too, indicates that a correct estimate of his character and achievement was gaining ground. It refers to the philanthropy of his administration in its promotion of the welfare of the people, and declares that the founding of Singapore 'secured to the British flag the maritime superiority of the Eastern Seas'. As the century went on his repute increased, as his achievement was seen in perspective, until today he has become an historical figure indissolubly connected with the transformation of the Far East.

It is not easy to get clear why the Court of the East India Company was so lacking in perception as to treat him no better than a troublesome subordinate. The Directors had available far more information about him than the general public, having received his despatches and debated his proceedings over so many years. They did not deny, as we have seen, the zeal that actuated him, the speed of his perceptions, the breadth of his mind, yet they withheld their whole-hearted support. Sophia in the last pages of her *Memoir* tries to throw light on this attitude. From the time of the Java expedition (1811) onwards, she says, 'Sir Stamford's course of duty forced him to act on his own responsibility. He asked for instructions and replies to his frequent references,' but these being delayed or not sent, he 'was impelled onwards by the course of events. Unfortunately, when his superiors did interfere, it was in general only to raise objections and to suggest a different course of measures, when, by their own delays, the time was passed in which their views could have been adopted.' And she concludes that the difference between their point of view and his arose 'more from their ignorance of the subjects on which they thought it necessary to decide than from any intention of being unjust or harsh towards the individual whose merits and services many of them, no doubt, justly appreciated'. If to this opinion one adds that the Directors were under pressure from the traditional policy of the Company, which was out of touch with novel conditions, and by the trend of affairs on the continent of Europe, one begins to see why they were not able to keep up with Raffles and accept his long views. They thought he was wrong, rash, disobedient, yet were given pause by the support he received by the Governors General, Minto and Hastings, and, hesitating to recall him, left him where he was, year after year. In the end, as their letter of 12 April 1826 shows, they came round to the conclusion that on the whole he had been right. But they found it impossible altogether to forgive him for having taken matters into his own hands, which, in their opinion, should have been settled in London, where what he achieved could have been attained more properly by diplomatic exchanges between heads of state.

Court's Settlement with Sophia

They were wrong in holding this opinion, for no committee could have done in London what Raffles was able to do on the spot, any more than a London committee could have won the battle of Waterloo. But as they did hold it, one can understand why they were in no mood to reward him for doing what, if left to themselves, they believed they would have done. Ungenerous though this attitude was to one who had undermined his health in their service, and who, while dying, continued to labour on their behalf, they might have lessened in some measure the censure of posterity had they taken the opportunity of his death to treat his widow in a handsome manner. But if some of the Directors were in favour of this course, the majority could not bring themselves to agree. Some fifteen thousand pounds were still owing on the bill of 12 April. The accounts department was instructed to go ahead and collect it from Raffles's estate.

What followed can be briefly related. In February 1827, seven months after Raffles's death, Sophia wrote to the committee of the Court expressing a desire for a final settlement of claims and asserting that she could not pay more than ten thousand pounds. Her capital, she said, amounted to £6,000 banked in Bengal, £2,400 in India stock and £1,150 in Consols, 'which will leave a balance of between five and six hundred pounds to make up the ten thousand'. On 7 March 1827 the Court agreed to accept the ten thousand pounds 'in satisfaction of all claims of the East India Company on the estate of the late Sir Thomas Raffles'. In short, the Directors took all her investments, leaving her, however, in possession of High Wood and its 112 acres of farmland. She appears also to have been able to retain 23 Lower Grosvenor Street until 1830 or later, when she disposed of the lease. For their clemency in letting her off the five thousand, the Directors deserve even less commendation than so stingy a reduction might conceivably have earned them, since two-thirds of the sum amounted to the expenses incurred by Raffles in founding Singapore, which he had drawn in the belief that they would be sanctioned by the Company. That the Company was now waiving its claim for repayment against his estate can hardly be called a concession, since Singapore, a place already worth millions to their China trade, had been acquired at such a bargain price. Altogether, one is obliged to say that the Court's treatment of Sophia was a piece of meanness hardly to be paralleled in history.

We have a glimpse of Sophia at Lower Grosvenor Street in June 1827. Travers called on her there and has in his *Diary*: 'I was surprised to find her so wonderfully cheerful and well.' Sophia was a woman of robust constitution and practical ability, ready to make the best of things. She was also very glad to see Travers, the faithful old friend of the family. He spoke feelingly of Raffles, 'my late never to be sufficiently regretted Friend, one who could not fail in attaching to him all with whom he was connected'. No man had warmer friends but throughout his life was unfortunate in arousing unfriendly feelings among persons whom he hardly knew and whom he had never intentionally harmed.

In January 1828 Travers records that Sophia asked him to help her write her *Memoir*. He was very happy to comply and contributed the extracts from his *Diary* which she included in her book. She wrote, however, a better English than he did and her narrative throughout, which she uses to connect the documents she publishes, shows no trace of his clumsier manner.

Later in 1828 he visited her at High Wood and spent some days collaborating over the *Memoir*. It was published in 1830. She continued to reside at High Wood, where she had Wilberforce as neighbour and friend until his death in 1833.

SOUTH-EAST ASIA

PHILIPPINE ISLANDS

MINDANAO

MOLUCCAS

CELEBES

China Sea

BORNEO

BALI

HAINAN

CHINA

Canton

COCHIN CHINA

JAVA

Borobudur

Jokyakarta

Batavia

SUMATRA

Palembang

Linga

Carimon

Rhio

Singapore

JOHORE

Malacca

Straits of Malacca

MALAYA

Penang

SIAM

ACHIN

Bencoolen

Straits

BURMA

Rangoon

INDIA

Calcutta

Indian Ocean

0   200   400   600   800
Miles

Her daughter Ella, sent home from Sumatra to save her life, only survived till the age of nineteen. As she was the last of his children, this meant that Raffles left no direct descendants. Sophia herself lived on till 1858, when she died at High Wood, aged seventy-two.

In some last reflections on Raffles's career, Travers wonders what he might have done, had he lived. Though very lucky at first in having Minto as his patron and being appointed Lieutenant-Governor of Java at thirty, he was pursued by ill luck thereafter. 'He was not able to do all the good he wished,' wrote Travers. A great friend of the Malay race, knowing their language well at a time when this was rare for an Englishman, he longed to deliver them from their servitude under the Dutch, and launch them as free individuals to make their way in the new world which was dawning for Asia. When the Islands were returned to the Dutch after Waterloo, his plans had to be abandoned. It was his bad luck that the requirements of European statecraft clashed with his humanitarianism. But though his major plans on behalf of the Malays could not materialize, his founding of Singapore prevented the Dutch from extending their mercantile system over the Malay states of the Peninsula, whose sultans saw their way in the course of the nineteenth century to a prosperous future under British guidance.

'Pity he was lost to his country at so early an age,' writes Travers. 'Much was expected of him.' A brilliant future surely awaited him, when in a more exalted official position, and with London opinion supporting him, he would build on the foundation he had laid. Death had carried him away on the threshold of yet greater achievements.

This was Travers's opinion and no doubt that of other friends.

But what more was there to do, what could he do to

surpass what he had done? He had opened the door, he had pointed to the path, he had provided the idea, he had performed the act. Singapore stood. What else was necessary? Born a giant, it was strong enough to come along by itself. So powerful were the dynamic forces which it unleashed that, had Raffles lived, he could have done little more than watch it grow at its own astounding pace. The stage was set for Europe's decisive incursion into East Asia. Old Asia was to disappear, a new Asia to be born, the Asia of the modern world. Such were the forces which Raffles set in motion by founding Singapore.

BIBLIOGRAPHY

BOULGER, DEMETRIUS CHARLES, *The Life of Sir Stamford Raffles* (London 1897)

BRYANT, ARTHUR, *The Age of Elegance 1812–1822* (London 1950)

BUCKLEY, C. B., *An Anecdotal History of Old Times in Singapore* (Singapore 1902) University of Malaya Press 1965

CRAWFURD, JOHN, *Journal of an Embassy to the Courts of Siam and Cochin China* (London 1829)

CURZON OF KEDLESTON, MARQUIS, *British Government in India* (London 1925)

EDWARDES, MICHAEL, *Asia in the European Age* (London 1961)

EGERTON, HUGH EDWARD, *Sir Stamford Raffles* (London 1900)

FARINGTON, JOSEPH, *Diary of*, edited by J. Greig (London 1922)

FURNIVALL, J. S., *Netherlands India* (Cambridge 1948)

HAHN, EMILY, *Raffles of Singapore* (New York 1946)

HALL, D. G. E., *The History of South East Asia* (London 1955)

HALL, D. G. E., *Atlas of South East Asia* (London 1964)

HAMILTON, Captain ALEXANDER, *New Account of East India* (Edinburgh 1727)

HARRISON, BRIAN, *South East Asia* (London 1960)

HASTINGS, MARQUIS OF, *Private Journal*, edited by the Marchioness of Bute (London 1858)

HICKEY, WILLIAM, *Memoirs* (London 1919)

LAMB, CHARLES, *Essays of Elia* (London 1823)

MAKEPEACE, W., and others, *One Hundred Years of Singapore* (London 1921) University of Malaya Press 1966

Bibliography

MARSDEN, WILLIAM, *History of Sumatra* (London 1811) Oxford University Press 1966

MILLER, HARRY, *The Story of Malaysia* (London 1965)

MINTO, COUNTESS OF, *Lord Minto in India* (London 1880)

M'LEOD, JOHN, *Voyage of the* Alceste *to Lewchew* (London 1818)

PARKINSON, C. NORTHCOTE, *East and West* (London 1963)

PHILLIPS, C. H., *The East India Company 1784–1834* (Manchester 1940)

PRATT, SIR JOHN, *The Expansion of Europe into the Far East* (London 1947)

RAFFLES, SOPHIA, LADY, *Memoir of the Life and Public Services of Sir Thomas Stamford Raffles* (London 1830)

RAFFLES, Sir THOMAS STAMFORD, *History of Java* (London 1817) Oxford University Press 1965

RAFFLES, THOMAS STAMFORD, B.A., *Memoirs of Rev. Thomas Raffles, D.D., LL.D.* (London 1864)

ROMEIN, JAN, *The Asian Century* (London 1962)

ROSEBERY, LORD, *Napoleon, the Last Phase* (London 1900)

RUNCIMAN, STEVEN, *The White Rajahs* (London)

STANHOPE, FIFTH EARL OF, *Conversations with the Duke of Wellington 1831–1857* (London 1888)

THOMSON, JOHN TURNBULL, *Translations from Hikayat Abdullah* (London 1874)

TREVELYAN, G. M., *British History in the Nineteenth Century* (London 1922)

WAKEHAM, Major ERIC, *The Bravest Soldier – Robert Rollo Gillespie* (Edinburgh 1937)

WILBERFORCE, R. I. and S., *Life of William Wilberforce* (London 1838)

WINSTEDT, Sir RICHARD, *Britain and Malaya* (London 1934)

WINSTEDT, Sir RICHARD, *Malaya and its History* (London 1948)

WURTZBURG, C. E., *Raffles of the Eastern Isles* (London 1954)

INDEX

Index

Index

Index

Index

Index

Books of Related Interest in Century Classics

William Franklin Sands
At The Court Of Korea
Undiplomatic Memories
Introduction by Christopher Hitchens
In the early 1890s Sands was sent by the US foreign service to Korea where he became the main adviser to the King until his dramatic ousting after two years.

Dymphna Cusack
Chinese Women Speak
First published in 1958 this book was the first in-depth study of Chinese women. The author spent eighteen months travelling over 7,000 miles through China, and interviewing hundreds of Chinese women from peasant to Manchu princess.

Ella Maillart
Forbidden Journey
Introduction by Dervla Murphy
Forbidden Journey is the story of a dream realised. In 1935, Ella Maillart set out in the footsteps of Marco Polo, from Peking to Kashmir, a journey said to be impossible for the Western traveller, certainly impossible for a woman. But Ella Maillart joined forces with Peter Fleming and together they crossed the Takla Makan Desert, climbed incredible mountain paths beside gorges of breaktaking beauty, riding sometimes on camels, sometimes on horseback. Visiting the forbidden Chinese fortress of Kashgaria and Sinkiang, they crossed the high plains of northern Tibet, the 'roof of the world'. Her account of the journey is 'enough to place her among the great travellers of the world'. (*Sunday Times*)

Richard Hughes
Foreign Devil
Thirty Years of Reporting from the Far East
From 1972 the Australian Richard Hughes was Hong
Kong correspondent for *The Times* and easily the most
well-known and colourful newspaper man in the Far
East. In a career spanning half a century he was the
shrewdest of China-watchers, and the Far East from
Singapore to Korea became his 'beat'. In 1956 Hughes
had achieved a spectacular coup when he obtained
exclusive interviews with Burgess and Maclean in
Moscow. Immortalized in fiction by John le Carré and
Ian Fleming, Hughes described *Foreign Devil* as consisting
of 'anecdotes and presumptions, excuses and reflections
spread over thirty years of great events'.

Isabella Bird
The Golden Chersonese
The Malay Peninsula is the setting for this classic of
Victorian travel writing by the courageous and intrepid
Isabella Bird, whose indomitable spirit took her to
remote and inhospitable corners of the earth.